Honey Steel's Gold

33 1/3 Global

33 1/3 Global, a series related to but independent from **33 1/3**, takes the format of the original series of short, music-based books and brings the focus to music throughout the world. With initial volumes focusing on Japanese and Brazilian music, the series will also include volumes on the popular music of Australia/Oceania, Europe, Africa, the Middle East, and more.

33 1/3 Japan

Series Editor: Noriko Manabe

Spanning a range of artists and genres – from the 1970s rock of Happy End to technopop band Yellow Magic Orchestra, the Shibuya-kei of Cornelius, classic anime series *Cowboy Bebop,* J-Pop/EDM hybrid Perfume, and vocaloid star Hatsune Miku – 33 1/3 Japan is a series devoted to in-depth examination of Japanese popular music of the twentieth and twenty-first centuries.

Published Titles:

Supercell's *Supercell* by Keisuke Yamada

AKB48 by Patrick W. Galbraith and Jason G. Karlin

Yoko Kanno's *Cowboy Bebop Soundtrack* by Rose Bridges

Perfume's *Game* by Patrick St. Michel

Cornelius's *Fantasma* by Martin Roberts

Joe Hisaishi's *My Neighbor Totoro: Soundtrack* by Kunio Hara

Shonen Knife's *Happy Hour* by Brooke McCorkle

Nenes' *Koza Dabasa* by Henry Johnson

Yuming's *The 14th Moon* by Lasse Lehtonen

Forthcoming Titles:

Yellow Magic Orchestra's *Yellow Magic Orchestra* by Toshiyuki Ohwada

Kohaku Uta Gassen: The Red and White Song Contest by Shelley Brunt

33 1/3 Brazil

Series Editor: Jason Stanyek

Covering the genres of samba, tropicália, rock, hip hop, forró, bossa nova, heavy metal and funk, among others, 33 1/3 Brazil is a series devoted to in-depth examination of the most important Brazilian albums of the twentieth and twenty-first centuries.

Published Titles:

Caetano Veloso's *A Foreign Sound* by Barbara Browning

Tim Maia's *Tim Maia Racional Vols. 1 &2* by Allen Thayer

João Gilberto and Stan Getz's *Getz/Gilberto* by Brian McCann

Gilberto Gil's *Refazenda* by Marc A. Hertzman

Dona Ivone Lara's *Sorriso Negro* by Mila Burns

Milton Nascimento and Lô Borges's *The Corner Club* by Jonathon Grasse

Racionais MCs' *Sobrevivendo no Inferno* by Derek Pardue

Naná Vasconcelos's *Saudades* by Daniel B. Sharp

Chico Buarque's First *Chico Buarque* by Charles A. Perrone

Forthcoming titles:

Jorge Ben Jor's *África Brasil* by Frederick J. Moehn

33 1/3 Europe

Series Editor: Fabian Holt

Spanning a range of artists and genres, 33 1/3 Europe offers engaging accounts of popular and culturally significant albums of Continental Europe and the North Atlantic from the twentieth and twenty-first centuries.

Published Titles:

Darkthrone's *A Blaze in the Northern Sky* by Ross Hagen

Ivo Papazov's *Balkanology* by Carol Silverman

Heiner Müller and Heiner Goebbels's *Wolokolamsker Chaussee* by Philip V. Bohlman

Modeselektor's *Happy Birthday!* by Sean Nye

Mercyful Fate's *Don't Break the Oath* by Henrik Marstal

Bea Playa's *I'll Be Your Plaything* by Anna Szemere and András Rónai

Various Artists' *DJs do Guetto* by Richard Elliott

Czesław Niemen's *Niemen Enigmatic* by Ewa Mazierska and Mariusz Gradowski

Massada's *Astaganaga* by Lutgard Mutsaers

Los Rodriguez's *Sin Documentos* by Fernán del Val and Héctor Fouce

Édith Piaf's *Récital 1961* by David Looseley
Nuovo Canzoniere Italiano's *Bella Ciao* by Jacopo Tomatis
Iannis Xenakis's *Persepolis* by Aram Yardumian
Vopli Vidopliassova's *Tantsi* by Maria Sonevytsky
Amália Rodrigues's *Amália at the Olympia* by Lila Ellen Gray

Forthcoming Titles:
Ardit Gjebrea's *Projekt Jon* by Nicholas Tochka
J.M.K.E.'s *To the Cold Land* by Brigitta Davidjants
Taco Hemingway's *Jarmark* by Kamila Rymajdo

33 1/3 Oceania

Series Editors: Jon Stratton (senior editor) and Jon Dale (specializing in books on albums from Aotearoa/New Zealand)
Spanning a range of artists and genres from Australian Indigenous artists to Maori and Pasifika artists, from Aotearoa/New Zealand noise music to Australian rock, and including music from Papua and other Pacific islands, 33 1/3 Oceania offers exciting accounts of albums that illustrate the wide range of music made in the Oceania region.

Published Titles:
John Farnham's *Whispering Jack* by Graeme Turner
The Church's *Starfish* by Chris Gibson
Regurgitator's *Unit* by Lachlan Goold and Lauren Istvandity
Kylie Minogue's *Kylie* by Adrian Renzo and Liz Giuffre
Alastair Riddell's *Space Waltz* by Ian Chapman
Hunters & Collectors's *Human Frailty* by Jon Stratton
The Front Lawn's *Songs from the Front Lawn* by Matthew Bannister
Bic Runga's *Drive* by Henry Johnson
The Dead C's *Clyma est mort* by Darren Jorgensen
Hilltop Hoods' *The Calling* by Dianne Rodger
Ed Kuepper's *Honey Steel's Gold* by John Encarnação
Chain's *Toward the Blues* by Peter Beilharz

Forthcoming Titles:
Screamfeeder's *Kitten Licks* by Ben Green and Ian Rogers
Luke Rowell's *Buy Now* by Michael Brown

Honey Steel's Gold

John Encarnação

Series Editors: Jon Stratton, UniSA Creative, University of South
Australia, and Jon Dale, University of Melbourne, Australia

BLOOMSBURY ACADEMIC
NEW YORK • LONDON • OXFORD • NEW DELHI • SYDNEY

BLOOMSBURY ACADEMIC
Bloomsbury Publishing Inc
1385 Broadway, New York, NY 10018, USA
50 Bedford Square, London, WC1B 3DP, UK
29 Earlsfort Terrace, Dublin 2, Ireland

BLOOMSBURY, BLOOMSBURY ACADEMIC and the Diana logo are trademarks
of Bloomsbury Publishing Plc

First published in the United States of America 2023
Reprinted 2023

For legal purposes the Acknowledgements on pp. xi–xii constitute an
extension of this copyright page.

Library of Congress Cataloging-in-Publication Data
Names: Encarnacao, John, author.
Title: Honey Steel's Gold / John Encarnação.
Description: [1st.] | New York : Bloomsbury Academic, 2023. |
Series: 33 1/3 Oceania | Includes bibliographical references and index. |
Summary: "A look at how Australian music legend Ed Kuepper dissolved
the boundaries between independent and mainstream sectors, and between
folk, rock and ambient musics, with his transcendent 1991 album Honey Steel's
Gold"– Provided by publisher.
Identifiers: LCCN 2022060971 (print) | LCCN 2022060972 (ebook) |
ISBN 9781501373350 (hardback) | ISBN 9781501373343 (paperback) |
ISBN 9781501373367 (ebook) | ISBN 9781501373374 (pdf) |
ISBN 9781501373381 (ebook other)
Subjects: LCSH: Kuepper, Ed. Honey Steel's gold. | Alternative
rock music–Australia–History and criticism. | Rock music–Australia–
1991–2000–History and criticism.
Classification: LCC ML420.K9495 E53 2023 (print) | LCC ML420.K9495
(ebook) | DDC 782.42166092–dc23/eng/20221221
LC record available at https://lccn.loc.gov/2022060971
LC ebook record available at https://lccn.loc.gov/2022060972

ISBN:	HB:	978-1-5013-7335-0
	PB:	978-1-5013-7334-3
	ePDF:	978-1-5013-7337-4
	eBook:	978-1-5013-7336-7

Series: 33 1/3 Oceania

Typeset by Integra Software Services Pvt. Ltd.
Printed and bound in Great Britain

For Zoë, even though she got to see Laughing Clowns
concerts back in the day and I didn't.

Contents

Note on the text

In preparation for this book, I interviewed Ed Kuepper, Adam Chapman, Mark Dawson and Martin Jennings in the first half of 2022. Any quotes from them not otherwise attributed come from these interviews.

At the risk of being pedantic, I am particular about using the correct names of bands, regardless of grammatical niceties. Thus The Saints are always The Saints, never the Saints, and Laughing Clowns are always Laughing Clowns, never the Laughing Clowns (though sometimes they might be the Clowns, especially as Kuepper himself uses that shorthand). I observe this rule for all band names.

Acknowledgements

This book was written on the never-ceded land of the Gadigal people of the Eora nation.

First, thanks to Jon Stratton for inviting me to pitch a book for this series and acknowledging the significance of Kuepper's contribution by saying yes to the suggestion of a volume on *Honey Steel's Gold*. Thanks also to Leah Babb-Rosenfeld at Bloomsbury New York for her understanding and encouragement, and to her colleagues for helping to shepherd this volume through.

Heartfelt thanks to Mark Dawson, Adam Chapman and Martin Jennings for taking time out for interviews, and especially to Ed Kuepper for his generosity and engagement in a series of interviews between February and September 2022. Thanks also to Tim Pittman at Feel Presents for initially putting me in touch with Ed, and for his support of the project.

Great appreciation is due to my early readers (and dear friends) Ryszard Dabek, Jonathan Hulme and Bernard Zuel for their insight and cheerleading, and especially to Stephen Creswell for a thousand conversations on all things Kuepper and his generosity with the lending of recorded and printed artefacts from his collection.

Thanks also to friends and colleagues for crucial conversations along the way, and in some instances, institutional support: Rachel Morley, Kate Fagan, Peter Marley, Matt McGuire, Ben Etherington, Alison Gill, Claire Coleman, Diana Blom, Jadey O'Regan, Tim Byron, Kenny Gormly, John O'Donnell, Bill Gibson, Hart Cohen, Bruce Crossman, Brendan Smyly and Clare Maclean.

I would also like to mention the supportive infrastructures of the Writing and Society Research Centre, Western Sydney University, the International Association for the Study of Popular Music (IASPM), and the School of Humanities and Communication Arts at WSU, under whose auspices I was the beneficiary of a research sabbatical during which I wrote the proposal and initial chapter outline of this book.

I'd like to thank Maria (mum), JJ (dad), Paris Mason, my sisters Linda, Liz, Adele and Anita, my brother Will and my aunts Evelyn and Chris for their faith in me. There is also Edie the Dog, who often insists on being helped up onto the couch behind me as I'm working at the desk, always ready with editorial cues, especially should I be eating toast or biscuits.

Last, but definitely not least, love always to Zoë Carides, who has aided the writing of this book in countless ways. Always my first reader, an eagle-eyed and perceptive proof-reader, she has engaged with theories and rants about the history of popular music for many years, and particularly about Ed Kuepper's various manifestations during the period of May-September 2022 during which this book was written. Thanks seems a tiny word in this context.

Acknowledgements

Track listing

1. King of Vice (9:51)
2. Everything I've Got Belongs to You (4:13)
3. Friday's Blue Cheer/Libertines of Oxley (8:01)
4. Honey Steel's Gold (5:21)
5. The Way I Made You Feel (5:18)
6. Not Too Soon (3:08)
7. Closer (but Disguised) (4:15)
8. Summerfield (3:36)

1 King of Vice

Honey Steel's Gold (1991) is a widescreen record. The watery piano theme that opens it gives way to groaning sounds with reversed envelopes which rise from the depths of both the piano and the pond on the album's cover. Drums ripple across the stereo picture along with layers of guitar processed in Ed Kuepper's signature style until the effect is orchestral. Mark Dawson's approach is all tom toms and cymbals, the snare-drum-with-snare-off serving as a kind of alto tom. There's something heraldic about such an approach to the drums, divorced as it is from the kick-snare-and-hats approach of pop and rock beats; heraldic in the sense of communicating across great distances. The reverberation that helps to define the soundscape of the whole record has the toms ricocheting off valleys and mountains. My imagination goes to the bucolic, to a pre-electric space. After an interlude of pure atmosphere, a second theme emerges, playing with the major and minor, delivered by a band of guitar things. Kuepper's twelve-string acoustic adds another element of wood and dirt. Notwithstanding the sounds flicking across the soundscape (ethereal electronic waifs we might assign to residual beliefs in the supernatural if we are to continue the feudal metaphor in this Kingdom of Vice) the twelve-string and tom toms combine in a sense of openness, woody-ness.

The second theme bears upon it, finally, The Voice: Kuepper with a watery delay. What has he to tell us? Not that he's the King of Vice exactly, but that it suits his partner to view him that way. As with so many of Kuepper's songs, the lyrics are suggestive rather than definitive. They entwine with the atmosphere of the sounds to encourage immersion and if not interpretation, a journey. The alleged King of Vice *plays* lion to his partner's lamb. We may infer that all is not what it seems.

'King of Vice' unfolds over ten minutes. It is magisterial. Some passages are melodic, with both the opening themes making returns, while other sections are more like sound pictures. The guitars, piano and drums are played improvisationally in the less melody-driven sections, even as the whole hangs together through an elusive harmonic scheme. The track eventually devolves into a rattling conversation between the drums and piano, winding down, arriving at a destination, or perhaps just running out of puff after such a long road.

None of the sections taken in isolation is complex, but their progression is both inevitable and somewhat unpredictable. This and the piece's length encourage surrender, and thus 'King of Vice' sets the tone for the record. It will be beautiful, powerful, enticing, but ultimately a puzzle impossible to solve. One that can be returned to over and over.

That inevitability of the structure of 'King of Vice' is a spectral Kuepper signature. The craft is to make the craft invisible, and across this album Kuepper achieves structures where the seams don't show. In fact, so carried away have I always been by the atmosphere and expansiveness of this piece of music that it is only now, thirty years into my relationship with it, that I've picked up the guitar and learned that the opening piano melody follows the same chord progression as the chorus. That is, part of the craft of the composition is simply that Kuepper has composed two melodies to the same set of chords. They meet only for the phrase 'king of vice', those notes played in the piano melody and sung in the chorus.[1] This sleight-of-hand is a disarming combination with the casual nature of Kuepper's vocal delivery, and the deliberately rough edges of his performances more broadly. Those rough edges are produced in this record (and others) as performative processes, which distract us from what is up Kuepper's compositional sleeve.

This is the claim to freedom from tighter arrangements made by *Today Wonder* (1990), a rejection of the well-rehearsed aesthetic of his late 1980s band The Yard Goes On Forever and *Everybody's Got To* (1988). *Today Wonder* snapped the cord of supposed refinement, development, pursuit of an industry standard. It's a live record – the title itself is a pun on 'two-day wonder', so quick was the recording. It is comprised of drums, guitar, some live processing and no further mixing (according to engineer Adam Chapman). *Honey Steel's Gold* adds Chris Abrahams on piano (it's his stately touch that sets the tone for the album) and takes the time to enhance the recordings with studio wonderment – atmospheres, processes. But it is wrong-headed to think of the production of the album as something *done* or *imposed* on the basic compositions or recordings. What we hear – the finished record – is the

---

[1] To dig further into the harmony, the open-endedness of the piece has as much to do with this chord progression as the track's epic length and the spaciousness of the arrangement. Most of the track marinates in a tonal centre of G; I use the term 'tonal centre' consciously, as modes both minor (vocal melody of the verses) and major (the passage from 2:00 onwards, and the recurring melody we first hear from 2:49) are invoked. But the introduction/chorus chord progression runs (all major chords, a bar of each): C – B♭ – F – C – E♭ – C – F – C. This progression never touches on the chord of G and flirts with C as home before seeming to resolve to F in the second last bar. Thus the home territory of G is disrupted again and again by a chord progression that wanders, but doesn't establish a new place to rest.

composition. The raw performances, pre-mixing, are not the artwork. The songs, pre-recording, are not the artwork. The artwork is the combination of all these things, including the sequencing of the tracks.

Suffice to say, beginning *Honey Steel's Gold* with 'King of Vice' is a masterstroke. Thinking about how to make the record marketable, one might have been inclined to kick off with something radio might have a nibble of – music radio was still very influential in 1991. And indeed, the early 1990s was the era of 'frontloading' albums with what the artist and label hoped might be hits. But thinking about the record as a work of art, 'King of Vice' throws down both the gauntlet and the welcome mat. In the words of Thurston Moore, it's a gesture of 'let's see who's here and who's not.'[2] It defers the gratification of the sorts of pleasures we have been taught to expect of pop music. But in its epic length, 'King of Vice' provides an environment to live in. It sets a comfortable pace. It suggests that playing the album will take us somewhere else for a period, rather than allowing us a few tourist snaps before changing the scenery every three or four minutes. It treats the listener as someone equal to the art, who does not need to be bribed with an instant hit of sugar; that's only ten minutes down the road in any case, in the shape of 'Everything I've Got Belongs to You'.

---

[2]   In the liner notes to Sonic Youth's compilation of outtakes *The Destroyed Room* (2006), where Moore says he is 'paraphrasing the inimitable Hair Police'.

2 A Book About an Album

Part 1: Honey Steel's Gold as Album Study

This book is about an album by Ed Kuepper. I might say ostensibly about an Ed Kuepper album, because ultimately any piece of writing is as much about itself and its author's preoccupations as it is about its apparent subject matter. Taking into consideration the various geographical tributaries of the franchise, at the time of writing there are over 200 titles in the 33 1/3 series. Each purports to be about an album, and fulfils that brief to a greater or lesser extent. What I'm going to do here is offer a quick survey of what seem to be the available options, and then give you the rationale for my choices.

In 1979, Greil Marcus edited the collection *Stranded: Rock and Roll for a Desert Island*.[1] We might think of this as the 'ur text' of album studies, as each essay is about an album chosen by its writer: the one album they would take to a desert island. Its contents split roughly fifty-fifty between those that pursue established journalistic tropes (some particular

---

[1] There is nothing to indicate that Marcus was referencing The Saints' 1976 debut single '(I'm) Stranded' in the title of this book, though it was conceived in 1978. Marcus does not mention The Saints in his later book on punk rock, *Lipstick Traces* (1989), though he did acknowledge them in his 'Real Life Rock' column in *Art Forum* in 1997.

to music journalism, some not) and those that embrace the so-called 'new journalism' to attempt something like a literary, or personal essay with the album chosen by the author as a kind of centre of gravity.

The 33 1/3 series adds to this mix works of academic analysis, as well as wildcards such as pieces of fiction that use a particular album as a jumping off point. In Marcus's book, the line between journalism and the literary is blurry; some of the most effective pieces of writing lie between these two states, or acquit both functions. I would venture that similarly, many, perhaps most of the 33 1/3 books do one of two things. Some offer a kind of 'procedural', a 'making of' – an investigation and chronology of how the album was made. This usually involves interviewing as many people who were involved with the project as possible for inside information: journalistic enquiry. The other mode is more analytical (literary or academic) and often involves the training of a big lens on the album: gender, race, place, sexuality, power, etc. Some of the books do both of these things.

The question that I might pose myself about contributing to this series of books is: how might I best serve the reader of a book about an Ed Kuepper album? Of course, this is nearly impossible to answer without assuming the homogeneity of the reading audience. Closer to home are questions not usually acknowledged, but of primary motivation to any writer: what kind of book am I comfortable writing? What kind of book do I have the ability to write? What sort of challenge do I want to set myself in writing this book? What kind of book would I like to read? If these questions seem selfish, this is only the case if a writer assumes themselves to be singular. Any writer or artist-practitioner works from a blind belief that something that satisfies them aesthetically will do the same for others;

that some kind of triangulation will occur in which the artefact, the author and the reader will meet.

What I'd like to do with this book has several components. I want to recontextualize *Honey Steel's Gold*, in terms of both Ed Kuepper's career and the state of the music industry in the early 1990s. I do think it is worth tracing, to some degree, how this record got to be made, while also thinking that on its own this is not enough. There's also something to be said for appraising the work: What are the terms under which it is best understood? What does it have to say to us, even if the answer to that question is not literal? How successful is it in realizing its apparent aims? But beyond these two frames, I think it is also worth surrendering to the record, and documenting that surrender. This is the experience that many listeners who love *Honey Steel's Gold* are familiar with, and to create a book about the album without engaging in this manner would be (I think) an omission.

So, some investigative, journalistic tools will be used. A handful of subjects was interviewed towards establishing the facts of the matter. An historical perspective on the album is offered. However, the usual façade of objectivity we find in both journalism and academic work is not projected here. There may be facts in terms of where and when the album was made, and who was involved, broader context in terms of Kuepper's career and the work of some of his contemporaries where relevant, but any telling of history is selective. I will undoubtedly leave out facts that seem crucial to others either because of my priorities or because they escaped me. Beyond the apparent facts, though, there will be interpretation, speculation and attempts to meet *Honey Steel's Gold* on its own terms in some imaginary place. That's where the gold is.

*

One of the central questions around writing a book like this is: can one really 'explain' a work of art? For centuries people have been trying. One way of thinking about this is an attempt to try to uncover the 'truth' around the making of the album. What was happening to the artist at the time personally? Who were the most important collaborators in the project? What equipment and locations were used? All of this is interesting, but it seems naïve to think that by amassing these and similar so-called 'facts' that we will shake free the significance of a work of art. We may understand certain elements of the context, but be no closer to the essence.

A common approach is to recount in detail the effect that an album had on the writer at an important juncture in their lives – usually the writer's vulnerable and formative teenage years. The value of this is that there has to be some universality to human experience, and that laying bare the effect a work has on an individual means there is potential for extrapolation to the experience of others, and maybe to elements of society more broadly if the work's reach is wide enough. The danger to this approach is that it can easily drift into solipsism – how much personal detail becomes too much information? Yes, any piece of writing is about the writer and can only come from their subject position, but at what point does this become tiresome for the reader? Perhaps it is a matter of style – if the writing is good enough, we will stay with the writer, and with any luck receive some kind of pay-off.

With respect to artists, including musicians, some kind of profile piece is also an option. So, it's not uncommon that an essay or book supposedly about an album becomes an extended piece on an artist's career, or on a particular set of circumstances that are (the argument would follow) expressed in a particular album.[2] In some examples, the album becomes only peripherally relevant – something to hang the thoughts the writer has on the artist's life, or supposed moral crisis on.

Yet another approach is to consider the environment that an album and artist resonates with, or helps to create. Beyond the 'big lenses' mentioned earlier, there are also the ways in which an album might challenge industrial structures and standards. It is in this space that we might measure the territory an album stakes out that is unfamiliar, and the impact it continues to have through generations; or more simply how it encapsulates its particular time.

So, this little book makes explicit the emphasis I've chosen to place on these various tropes of album studies. As there has been no book on Ed Kuepper to this point (a fact I find surprising given his significance), I think that contextualization is necessary. I will recount this from two perspectives: the context of Kuepper's career, some fifty years in duration at the time of writing if we consider that The Saints were formed in 1973; and the music industry in which *Honey Steel's Gold* was released (or perhaps more specifically the relationship between industrial concerns, Kuepper's career, and this album specifically). I would think that I am not the only one curious about how the album was made, so a 'making of' chapter is included, though it might not follow the usual frameworks.

Complementary to this supposed fact-gathering will be chapters that attempt to grapple with *Honey Steel's Gold* as

---

2   Reflecting the background of many of the writers in journalism, the artist-profile-disguised-as-album-essay accounts for six of the twenty essays in Marcus's *Stranded*: those on The Velvet Underground, Jackson Browne, Huey 'Piano' Smith, Neil Young, Linda Ronstadt and The '5' Royales.

artwork. What is it doing, what are its effects, how does it affect us (or I suppose, me)? I will not attempt to prescribe meaning but rather try to share the aesthetic experience of the album as a point of connection or intersection between the music, myself as the author, and the reader. For the most part, this will be delivered as short essays on each track on the album.

Any great work of art – and the fact that I am writing a book about *Honey Steel's Gold* does mean that I hold it in high esteem – is at some point unfathomable. It must also be inexhaustible, or else we will have no reason to continue to return to it. If it is an object, it is so multi-faceted that we can perceive only a limited number of its facets at any one time. My feeling is that album studies that concentrate too exclusively on the making of the album, or the personal life of the artist (among other supposedly objective concerns) are content to look at a single reflective surface. We may get to know that plane extremely well, but ultimately this is a limited view of the work. Within the space available, I've attempted to engage with as many aspects of *Honey Steel's Gold* as I can, or at least to turn it over in my mind until I can present it to you in something like three dimensions.

Part 2: Ed and Me[3]

Around the time I turned fourteen, right at the end of 1978, I caught the train to the city from Sydney's western suburbs with my friend Bill to visit Phantom Records. It was my first visit

---

[3]   The passage that follows is not so much 'the writer's vulnerable and formative teenage years' – though these do get a brief look-in – as an outline of my subject position, necessary in terms of rejecting any façade of impartiality or omniscience.

to an 'import store' where, I had learned, I could find records not available through the usual channels. It felt very grown up, especially the part where I defied my mother to make the trip (incurring a penalty of being grounded for two weeks, which I don't think stuck). I selected four import singles, probably all I could afford, talismans of a potential identity: Public Image Limited's debut, 'Public Image', then brand-new in the fold-out newspaper cover; Sex Pistols''God Save the Queen'; Devo's 'Jocko Homo'/'Mongoloid'; and the UK edition of The Saints' '(I'm) Stranded' on the Power Exchange label. Another friend of mine had a US copy of the second Saints album *Eternally Yours*, which I borrowed. I was fascinated to discover it was as full of melody and reflection as noise and anger. After all, out in the 'burbs we were chasing the punk zeitgeist. We scratched around for the few clues that randomly fell on us, so far from the world's apparent cultural centres, glimpsed on TV and at record shops. *RAM* magazine was about as good as it got.[4] So began my relationship with Ed Kuepper's music.

As much as I dug The Saints, Kuepper's next band, Laughing Clowns, didn't really cross my radar at the time. This is to my enduring regret, as I love their music so much. I never got to see them play live. Although still 14 when they first played, I was 19–20 when they last toured, so I feel I have no excuse except not being cool enough. Somehow, I rediscovered Kuepper soon after. Laughing Clowns' final album, *Ghosts of an Ideal Wife* and Kuepper's debut solo album, *Electrical Storm*, are formative Kuepper records for me. Both released in 1985, they're the ones I discovered for myself, that are foundational to

---

[4]   *Rock Australia Magazine (RAM)* was published fortnightly from
     1975 to 1989. I bought it religiously from about 1978 and, starting
     with an unsolicited review of a Hoodoo Gurus gig, had writing
     published there from 1985 until the magazine's demise.

the way I understand and respond to Kuepper as an artist, and the point from which I determinedly worked my way through his back-catalogue. *The History of Rock and Roll Vol. 1* (1984), a compilation of Clowns material from 1980 to 1983, was another purchase around that time, and a great primer.

I went to see Ed play live as often as possible in the period 1985–7, but fell out of the habit with his third album *Everybody's Got To*. There was something about the production that held me at arm's length. I was fully immersed in the American post-hardcore of the likes of Meat Puppets and Firehose, and local noise absurdists like Thug and Lubricated Goat, and attempting to work in the same universe with my own band Smelly Tongues (with the same Bill from the Phantom Records visit). Big snare drums with heaps of reverb were a red rag; novel in the early 1980s, by the end of the decade they were tired. Even today, I can hardly listen to The Triffids' *Calenture* (1987) for the same reason. Like many, I was brought back into the fold with the minimalist, yet sensual reset of *Today Wonder*, and kept enthralled with the run of albums that followed, which included *Honey Steel's Gold* and *Black Ticket Day* (1992). At the same time, Kuepper released two studio albums by the rock trio-as-blowtorch project The Aints, which were hungrily received and duly cranked by me.

Although very few could keep up with the torrent of releases Kuepper unleashed in the second half of the 1990s, I bought many of them, and others came my way through music journalism. I appreciated the combination of sonic variety and unambiguous authorial signatures: certain harmonic and melodic structures, often tropes of folk and blues-derived rock; a combination of restraint and expansiveness; a sense of wry and sometimes dark humour; a pitiless eye on the human condition that, often as not, was trained inward. All of these elements are found in *Honey Steel's Gold*. In fact, I see it as the fulcrum and microcosm of Kuepper's work, a stunning distillation of everything that makes him special.

Eventually, I did become bewildered by the pace and frequency of late 1990s releases. Although I loved experimental instrumental albums such as *Starstruck* (1996) and *The Blue House* (1997), the albums of new songs petered out. By the time *Smile … Pacific* arrived (2000), I wasn't paying attention. I still went to see Kuepper perform semi-regularly, but with dozens of recorded artefacts of the man's work in my collection didn't feel it was necessary (nor possible, really) to be a completist.

How silly I was. As I write this, I am listening to Kuepper's *The Return of the Mail-Order Bridegroom*, a 2014 live-in-the-studio album recorded in three days. It features a mix of Saints, Clowns and solo career tunes and three covers, including a lovely, understated tilt at Tom Rush's 'No Regrets'. One might pick it up at the merch desk of a gig of Kuepper's or find it online and think – doesn't look essential, I have most of these songs already.

You'd be wrong. Although he has released many records like this – either live or studio remakes of old material – they each cast a spell. On this Saturday morning in Marrickville in Sydney's inner west, my second cup of tea cooling at the dining room table, Ed's steady right hand chopping at his guitar, or picking like a folky old bluesman, his voice turning fragments of a life over and over … the space is warmed, Ed is here having a yarn, he could almost be sitting at the other side of the table with his own cuppa.

And now on to the aforementioned *Starstruck*, subtitled *Music for Films and Adverts*, a set of twenty-eight miniatures that straddle the acoustic and the electronic, some subsisting on wisps of melody or mechanistic rhythms, some unashamedly romantic in a kind of midday movie way. It's a fascinating journey at the edges of the Kuepper canon, the rudiments of his style left to run without the fetters of song structure, tracks sometimes unceremoniously cut off or faded out after less than a minute.

Kuepper is one of that handful of artists that, in one of his many manifestations, is never far from my stereo. Seldom a week will go by without Ed's voice resonating throughout the house. And about that voice: some might find it an acquired taste. It tends to the undemonstrative; sometimes it has a sleepy quality, at others a sense of rueful self-reflection. It is not traditionally beautiful, or powerful, or virtuosic. Like much about Kuepper's music, it doesn't pander. It's a bit take-it-or-leave-it.

Yet it is a sound of comfort for those who have found nourishment in Kuepper's music for decades. Its singer-songwriter idiosyncrasy is a trademark of quality. There is much beauty and wonder to be found in Kuepper's music: in the deathless melodies he spins out of his guitar like living entities, encapsulating the moods and emotions of his compositions. But the voice. That's where he meets us toe to toe, and as we hear his human frailty we see him, we see ourselves, we see each other, animals with oversized brains, sweating and worrying, finding relief where we can, looking up at the sky and down into the water, wondering at the magnificence and loveliness and indifference of it all.

3 Everything I've Got Belongs to You

As much as it is a well-crafted pop song and singalong, 'Everything I've Got Belongs to You' consolidates something about Kuepper's apparent worldview, or perhaps his projection of same. The track comes across as a beatific ballad, all major chords and easy melodies, but rather than the lyrics sharing this outlook they carve through it with bad temper and discontent. The first lines are 'I have designs on you that come from dirty books/And I'd lie to you if that was what it took'. Naked lust, and a readiness for deception. The bridge: 'I don't care who's wrong or right/I'd just start another fight'. Pure belligerence. And the final verse, the classic lines 'Now time has proved I'm churlish and I'm rude/And I find a real contentment in bad moods.' He sounds like quite the catch. In isolation, the refrain of 'everything I've got belongs to you' seems a declaration of fidelity and permanence, but in the context of the rest of the lyric it's a kind of blackmail, a rationale, an alibi. In this juxtaposition of sweet music and sour lyric, pulled together with a title that without further listening may ring romantic, 'Everything I've Got Belongs to You' has something in common with the Police's 'Every Breath You Take' (stalker!) and R.E.M.'s 'The One I Love' (where the beloved of the title is 'a simple prop', soon discarded). Each very different to the other, but each a booby-trap for the inattentive wedding planner.

Another way to look at this lyric, especially in the context of the serenity of the music, is that it portrays a kind of disarming honesty: I'm not pretending to be anything other than a grumpy pain in the arse, not even particularly honest: will you have me? The song makes no accusations of the romantic other to whom it is addressed. It's warts-and-all and cap-in-hand. It's a riposte to the anodyne love songs that are so far from the everyday negotiations and humilities of long-term relationships, and the music serves as a Trojan horse for the medicine.

That's the beauty of a song: in a four-minute package, the songwriter posits a character or situation for the singer to inhabit. Though no doubt built from the songwriter's experiences and observations, it is an assemblage that resonates outwards into the experiences and observations of the listener. We can each relate to it in our own way – in the case of 'Everything I've Got', as the cap-in-hander not feeling worthy of the indulgence of our partner; as the unapologetic, ill-tempered, manipulative partner; as the significant other on the receiving end of these postures; as all of these at once; and of course many other options born of the listener's specific perspective.

I'm not suggesting that we map this song onto Kuepper's personality. However, I do believe that a song such as this contributes to his persona. A fan of Kuepper's work will subconsciously link 'Everything I've Got' to the late-period Clowns tune 'New Bully in Town', to the later solo track 'Wasn't I Pissed Off Today', and most of all to Kuepper's onstage persona. When relaxed, Kuepper playfully chastises and teases the audience. He seems to find a real contentment in playing the curmudgeon – with a big smile on his face, secure that the audience is in on the joke. He sometimes pretends to take us for granted while engendering a great warmth. In the two shows I saw on Kuepper's 2022 tour with Jim White, they encored with 'Everything I've Got Belongs to You', Ed instigating a crowd singalong with varying levels of success (small-town Milton more forthcoming than self-conscious Sydney). It's not difficult to feel he is singing this churlish love song to his audience: time has proved I'll play what I want, when I want. I'm an artist who follows inspiration, and that might mean you get an instrumental album when you'd like some songs, or a guitar that sounds like some bizarre electronic harp that complicates your reception of the songs you came to hear ... but I do understand that it is because of your loyalty that I continue to make a living. Transposed to the artist-audience relationship, the song seems to say 'thanks for hanging in there with me, I know the ride's been rocky at times. Everything I have's because of you, dear people beyond the footlights.'

4 Kuepper and Historiography

Ed Kuepper has been hiding in plain sight for decades. That's not quite right; he's been an active and unique player in the Australian cultural ecosystem for almost fifty years but, it seems to me, is mostly remembered for the first five of those. When I interviewed Kuepper in 2006, he felt that his career post-The Saints had largely been written out of the history of Australian rock music. He was not impressed, and I didn't blame him.[1] In reality, Kuepper formed Laughing Clowns in 1979. It remains one of the most original and intriguing groups Australia has ever produced. There were multiple releases of their records in the UK, where they were based for a couple of periods, and across Europe, where they toured more than once. After numerous line-up changes, they petered out as 1984 turned into 1985, upon which Kuepper's solo career began.

The early-mid 1980s is a remarkable period for Australian independent music and its international impact. In the wake

---

[1] A case in point was the ABC miniseries *Long Way to the Top* (2001). To be fair, this had something to do with the historical skew of the six-part series, where the first four episodes cover 1956–81, and with a slight overlap, the last two episodes cover 1976–2000. We might say this is typical boomer historiography, with the 'golden era' of rock and roll through to punk/new wave getting priority, and the latter period being not so much skirted over as picked through. Of course, the further back something is, the easier it is to assess it.

of The Saints' (and Radio Birdman's) relocation to London, a succession of Australian groups tried their luck over there. Most prominently we hear about The Birthday Party (and their singer Nick Cave's solo career), The Go-Betweens and The Triffids in this context.[2] Laughing Clowns, with their jazz-influenced post-punk and Kuepper's *particular* voice, are perhaps harder to grasp than the others, though their 'Eternally Yours' (1984) is a classic of the period equal in stature to The Go-Betweens' 'Cattle and Cane' (1983) and The Triffids' 'Wide Open Road' (1986). They're often left out of histories of the period, perhaps because their story isn't as headline-worthy as the self-destructive self-styled polymath Cave, the genius-life-cut-short of The Triffids' David McComb, the soap-opera of the intra-band relationships of The Go-Betweens, or even the spectacular evolution and explosion of the original Saints.[3] Certainly Kuepper did not bask in notoriety as did Cave, did not have the smooth voice and pop hooks of The Go-Betweens' Grant McLennan, nor the press-ready foppishness of McLennan's partner Robert Forster, though he may have shared something of the forthrightness of Go-Betweens drummer Lindy Morrison. Laughing Clowns were never the flavour of the month with the influential British music press the way The Triffids were in 1984–5.

Between Laughing Clowns and the early 1990s, Kuepper released three solo albums; the third (*Everybody's Got To*) was

---

[2]   The Triffids were a bit later. A(n incomplete) chronology of the exodus of Australian bands of the post-punk era to London would run something like: The Saints, 1977; Radio Birdman, 1978; The Go-Betweens briefly in 1979–80, then 1982; The Birthday Party, 1980; Laughing Clowns, 1982; The Moodists, 1983; Hunters and Collectors, 1983; Scientists, 1984; Severed Heads, 1984; The Triffids, 1984.

[3]   That's not to disparage any of these groups. The real estate each has claimed in my record collection continues to nourish me.

issued by Capitol in the United States and tentacles of EMI globally. Through 1986–9, Kuepper toured tirelessly with his group, The Yard Goes On Forever (henceforth, as Kuepper refers to them and this period, The Yard). They were often on Australian TV performing various singles. Though not scoring a proper mainstream hit, 'Also Sprach the King of Eurodisco' (1986 – catchy title, right? Why didn't it catch on?) and 'Not a Soul Around' (1987) were sizable indie hits. Again, aside from Kuepper's loyal fanbase, for whom he tours in various configurations several times a year, this period seems largely forgotten.

The period of the early 1990s was one of upheaval in the music industry. Ratcat (locally), and then six months later Nirvana (internationally) spearheaded a collision of independent and major labels in 1991–2 that would transform the way business was done. The Australian manifestation of this phenomenon is well documented by Craig Mathieson in *The Sell-In* (2000) with, to my mind, a notable omission. Ed Kuepper's *Honey Steel's Gold* broke through to the Australian top forty while remaining entirely independent. Maybe that's the reason it and Kuepper are missing-in-action in Mathieson's book – neither illustrates an aspect of independent music getting into bed with the majors. But it is significant that this was the first of a string of top fifty albums for Kuepper, and also significant that his contribution to the storming of the record-chain-store barricades remains largely undocumented.

This potted history, of which there will be more detail in the coming pages, only covers the first two decades of Kuepper's career; roughly from the mid-1970s to the mid-1990s. Many more chapters have unfolded over the ensuing twenty-five years: various solo manifestations, the power trio of The Aints in the early 1990s, the expanded The Aints![4] in the late 2010s, and recently the improvising quartet Asteroid Ekosystem. For now, let's consider some reasons that Kuepper hasn't always been given his due, beyond those early years.

We might start with straightforward ageism. How can the story of the modest commercial breakthrough of someone's umpteenth album (*Honey Steel's Gold* being Kuepper's fifth solo LP after three with The Saints and three with the Clowns) be as sexy as that of the hot young things in their first flush of inspiration and daring? Spiderbait, Regurgitator, Ratcat and Clouds are all stars of Mathieson's narrative. And over in the old corner in their mid-to-late thirties, Kuepper and Dave Graney and Kim Salmon, patron saints of post-punk who apparently had their shot at infamy a decade previously.[5]

Another is the neatness and headline-worthiness of The Saints' story: the band from Brisbane who invented punk rock in isolation from, but roughly at the same time, as the Ramones in New York City. The band whose self-released single caused shockwaves in the UK music press in late 1976 and resulted in EMI UK ordering their Australian arm to sign this band they'd never heard of. The band who represented disenfranchised youth in the context of Joh Bjelke-Petersen's

---

[4]   Kuepper added the exclamation mark for the 2017–19 iteration of the band, going so far as to refer to them as 'The Aints exclamation mark' in interviews.

[5]   Graney and Salmon had each burnt out early bands in London in the mid-1980s – The Moodists and Scientists respectively. Each would later achieve greater success: Salmon with The Beasts of Bourbon (especially in Europe) and Graney with high mainstream domestic sales and profile in the mid-1990s with Dave Graney 'n' the Coral Snakes.

police state of Queensland (a true punk story!).[6] The band with an incredible three-album arc that climaxed with one of the first albums we might call post-punk (*Prehistoric Sounds*, 1978). Never mind that Kuepper continues to reject the label of punk for The Saints. It's worth remembering that Kuepper was not the singer of The Saints, but the guitarist and co-songwriter with singer Chris Bailey. Bailey carried on with the name after the demise of the initial band, resulting, in the 1980s at least, in brand-identification of The Saints as Bailey's outfit, and a division between Kuepper fans, many of whom for which the early Saints is the only Saints,[7] and Bailey fans, for whom Bailey was the only constant.

We might also say that Kuepper has never been one for cultivating an image. While his followers appreciate his strong personality – his dry humour, self-deprecation, way with language, uncompromising views, not to mention his addictive musical signatures – few beyond dedicated music fans would be able to pick him out of a line-up of 1980s Australian rockers. We might think of Chrissy Amphlett's schoolgirl-on-a-rampage; Michael Hutchence's writhing sex-leopard; Nick Cave's gothic preacher. Despite his brief dalliance with eyeliner at the tail end of the Yard period, Kuepper has always been about the music. Promotional photographs of him span a compact continuum from elegant to slightly dishevelled (but not enough to make a statement). Maximum authenticity, genuine rather than

---

[6] Though this reads well, it doesn't *quite* match reality, as I'll discuss later on.

[7] Although I like some of the songs Chris Bailey wrote and recorded as The Saints after Kuepper's departure, I am one of those people; if I say 'The Saints', I am talking about the Kuepper period, what Kuepper on his YouTube channel refers to as 'The Saints 1973–78'.

contrived; fairly minimal cut-through beyond the converted. The film clip for Kuepper's 1992 single 'Real Wild Life' tells the story. Dear Ed seems to be trying his best to be a pop singer in the wake of the breakthrough of 'The Way I Made You Feel' but doesn't seem capable of a smile or of much expression at all. The dancing girls around him make him look even more out of place. I love this video for its presentation of an artist that won't, possibly can't be assimilated. He's our Ed, the perpetual outsider.

Further to all of this, I would contend that Kuepper's musical style is at once inimitable and rather subtle. Despite the feisty guitars that saw the early Saints equated with punk, and the wayward horns that meant Laughing Clowns do fit somewhat in the stylistic expanses of post-punk, his work since 1985 is kind of 'rootsy'. That is to say, essentially he is a singer-songwriter with a basis in the blues and Anglo-American folk, with odd flecks of country. Another way to think of this is that his creative capacities were initially developed during his teen years, when the pop and rock of the late 1960s and early 1970s helped set reference points like heavy rock, the singer-songwriter, and pop both grand and silly. He is a quintessential rock artist, in that his electric guitar-based practice is somewhat omnivorous. As *Honey Steel's Gold* demonstrates so beautifully, Kuepper can take a structure of relative harmonic simplicity for an epic turn within a lush soundscape. For all the genre-words I've dropped here, it's impossible to define the style of the album. Like much great music, it is ineffable. It cannot really be translated into words, only experienced. Eluding identification by genre-label, the album and its creator further escape tellings of history that rely on easy categories.

Conversely, we might say that for all of its roots in blues, folk and singer-songwriter tropes, the timbres and sonic signatures of Kuepper's catalogue of recordings might be bewilderingly diverse to the uninitiated or unadventurous. The overdriven guitars that define The Saints return and are blasted into orbit for the Aints records of the early 1990s, but they are very different in character to the fusion of acoustic and electric timbres on Kuepper's classic singer-songwriter solo debut *Electrical Storm* (1985). In the mid-1990s Kuepper began experimenting with a guitar synthesizer. On a live solo record like *With a Knapsack on my Back* (1997) the songs are transformed by sounds it is unlikely you have heard a guitar make before. It's not exactly avant-garde, but it's also not like rock or folk or singer-songwriter records you'd be familiar with. Then there's a record like *The Blue House* (1997) – instrumental, somewhat electronic in a lo-fi manner, wonderful on its own terms. But one can imagine a fan of *Honey Steel's Gold* or The Saints buying it speculatively and thinking 'what the fuck is this?' On one hand, Kuepper is a traditionalist, a roots music artist difficult to further pigeonhole. On the other, his musical wanderlust makes him elusive for different reasons.

5 Friday's Blue Cheer/ Libertines of Oxley

Kuepper is an explorer and navigator, a cartographer of the electric guitar. It's something he's not given enough credit for. Anyone who has seen him perform over the years will have some sense of this, even if it's an aspect of his art that is somewhat underplayed. There are no physical gestures that signpost his particular kind of virtuosity – no foot on monitor wedge, no guitar-face as he wails into a technically demanding solo. Certain types of guitar-playing virtuosity have become such clichés in rock music – along the continuum from the blues licks of Eric Clapton to any number of heavy metal hijinks – that genuine exploration like Kuepper's flies under the radar. I am loath to compare Kuepper to anyone much but Neil Young does come to mind. While I don't believe he is 'influenced' by Young, Young is another artist who has doggedly pursued the possibilities of guitar *tone* and expression while rejecting the clichés of rock guitar virtuosity.[1]

For Kuepper's work is in extending the timbral range of the guitar, and in using the guitar to create sonic environments. It is never about how many notes he can play in a bar, about modal complexity or transpositions. He is not a jazz player, and from this perspective one might appreciate Kuepper's lack of

---

[1] It's tempting to think of The Aints as Kuepper's Crazy Horse, though I think this would be to conveniently forget the timbral and stylistic multiplicity of those albums released under the name Ed Kuepper.

patience for those who refer to Laughing Clowns as jazz-rock, or free jazz. Mahavishnu Orchestra or Ornette Coleman it ain't. This is possibly why Asteroid Ekosystem – the collaboration between the Alister Spence Trio and Kuepper – works so well: Spence, Lloyd Swanton and Toby Hall, as much as being jazz musicians and speaking that language fluently, lean into timbral exploration.

'Friday's Blue Cheer/Libertines of Oxley' is a case in point. It is built upon similar rumbling-across-the-plains tom work by Mark Dawson as 'King of Vice', yet with a different tempo and a different feeling. The textures are created entirely by percussion and guitars. *Today Wonder* set these coordinates for a certain type of musical adventure, minimalist yet rich with timbral detail.

And so with 'Friday's Blue Cheer/Libertines of Oxley', as with much of *Honey Steel's Gold* we have a bedrock of twelve-string acoustic guitar. In fact, it's two layers of twelve-string, the first clear of effect, chugging away, the other with some reverb adding melodic material. A third, electric guitar is the star turn, with coruscating distortion and liberal sprinklings of piercing harmonics. Ed is jamming across these three parts, exploring the space, seeing how much can be done with a bare minimum of harmonic material; in his hands it is quite a lot.

Blue Cheer, name-checked in the song's title, was a San Francisco band of the late 1960s who were perhaps the heaviest sound of their time – for rock music, anyway. Their first two albums were released in 1968, which means they pip Black Sabbath and the Stooges by a year. Neck and neck with Led Zeppelin perhaps, but not as in debt to, or as fluid in blues tropes and playing. Their stuff is *raw*. Jimi Hendrix … well, you might have me there, though again we're talking about an overloaded blues. The earliest version of The Saints, Kid

Galahad and the Eternals, apparently covered a couple of Blue Cheer songs, so it would seem it is a tribute of sorts.[2] In terms of 'Friday's Blue Cheer/Libertines of Oxley' though, the mention of Blue Cheer seems a red herring, the track having more to do with the fuzz haze and relentless motion of The Aints' *Ascension*, recorded about the same time.

And what about the other half of the name: the Libertines of Oxley? Oxley as in the family that spawned brothers Jeremy and Peter of the Sunnyboys? Peter has played bass with Kuepper in various formations over the last twenty years, and sister Melanie sang backing vocals all through Kuepper's 1987 album *Rooms of the Magnificent*. Well, probably not. Oxley is the suburb of Brisbane where Kuepper grew up, and it also gives its name to the Oxley Creek Playboys, one of Kuepper's bands of the late 1990s. So, if The Saints took shape in the Kuepper family's garage,[3] it stands to reason that it is in fact they who are the Libertines of Oxley. This would seem to have nothing at all to do with the lyric, which describes a kind of love triangle that the singer/protagonist is at the losing corner of.

It's quite possible I'm missing something … but a title that throws out two evocative allusions only to confuse is a typically Kuepper caper. See also 'Honey Steel's Gold' in a couple of chapters' time …

Storey, 'Ed Kuepper', 11.

As per Kuepper's liner notes to the 1995 archival Saints CD release *The Most Primitive Band in the World: The Saints Live from the Twilight Zone, Brisbane 1974*.

Friday's Blue Cheer/Libertines of Oxley

29

6 Journey to *Honey Steel's Gold*

The Saints – Rejecting, Surviving and Transcending Punk

In 2008, I wrote a piece called 'Bastard Country, Bastard Music: The Legacy of Punk in Australia'. I've always been more interested in what I call punk aesthetics than punk rock *per se*, and argued that certain Australian groups – the Kuepper-era Saints, X, The Birthday Party, the Drones, Kiosk – are relevant to this conversation. Each embodied and often wrote from the perspective of the outsider, which I suggested 'has particular resonance in a society descended from convicts and migrants with no legitimate claim to the land ... Rather than a stereotypical punk sound and image, [these artists] reject the punk label by creating singular styles.'[1] Paradoxically, this is what I think of as the essence of punk; it has more to do with an attitude of disaffection, a rejection of available options both musically and industrially, than a style of music.

The Saints' debut single '(I'm) Stranded' (1976) delivers a sound and attitude, as well as emerging at a point in time, where an identification of the record as punk rock is logical. But as Kuepper will always point out, it was a sound that was developed in relative isolation in Brisbane. Yes, Kuepper and

---

[1]   Encarnação, 'Bastard Country, Bastard Music', 201.

co-conspirators Chris Bailey and Ivor Hay were motivated to some extent by the raw power of the Stooges and the rock 'n' roll abandon of the New York Dolls, which places them in the company of many contemporaries who also found alternatives in those records. But, forming as Kid Galahad and the Eternals in 1973 and changing their name to The Saints the following year, their sound was fully formed before they had heard a note of the Ramones or Sex Pistols.[2]

In 'Bastard Country', I propose that '(I'm) Stranded' is

> a cry of alienation from a colonial outpost, of disconnection from other points of origin, written by two immigrants, Chris Bailey (from Ireland) and Ed Kuepper (from Germany). The alienation of the song is non-specific, but there are inferences of a place and society which has little to offer …[3]

As I will discuss in the following chapter, there are specific reasons why Brisbane in the mid-1970s might be such a place, but for the moment I want to think about Kuepper's migrant origins. As an interviewee, Kuepper is nothing if not consistent, and one of those modes of consistency is his absolute rejection of the idea of any of his musical ventures belonging to any scene or style. The singularity of his musical vision is a source of particular pride, and this intertwines with his 'churlish and rude' persona. (I say persona because, it seems to me, in actuality he is neither of these things). For one of many possible examples, Kuepper writes that his decision to include an alternate mix of 'Eternally Yours' on every edition of

---

[2] This claim of Kuepper's is backed up by the audio evidence of the aforementioned CD *The Most Primitive Band in the World: The Saints Live from the Twilight Zone, Brisbane 1974*.

[3] Encarnação, op. cit., 204.

the Laughing Clowns album *Law of Nature* (1984) after the first vinyl pressing was one of 'sheer bloody-mindedness'.[4] Even the title of the compilation this comment comes from, *Cruel, But Fair* sends the same message: take it or leave it.

So while I understand Kuepper's reluctance to be associated with punk – The Saints did their own thing, they didn't follow a trend or jump on a bandwagon – I wonder whether this outsider stance comes from a deeper place. In a recent interview, Kuepper mentions that, having emigrated from Germany with his parents when he was 'three or so', upon starting school he did not speak English.[5] I was born in Australia and grew up speaking English but share with Kuepper a migrant background. Although I found friends, I was as a matter of course made to feel outside of the norm due to my surname; and if I suffered from discrimination as a 'wog' on the outskirts of Sydney in the 1970s, I would think there was some of that to Kuepper's experience growing up in the suburbs of Brisbane in the 1960s. It's a common story that artists of any stripe feel special, or outside of society, but each of us has our own path to this. One way of coping with structures that don't recognize you is to reject them before they can reject you, and this seems to be Kuepper's default position with respect to music scenes and movements.

The initial flush of The Saints' success in 1976–7 was ironic; their seat at the table was due to the fact that '(I'm) Stranded' represented a zeitgeist that had already been recognized by those interested in vernacular musical cultures in the cultural centres of New York and London. It was John Ingham – one of those cultural scouts, writing for England's *Sounds*

---

4   Kuepper, 'Blow by Blow'.

5   Wilsteed, 'John Wilsteed chats with Ed Kuepper', 3:00–3:30.

magazine – that declared it 'Single of This and Every Week' in the issue dated 16 October 1976, and in so doing changed the lives of these young Brisvagrants.[6] 'We're not punks!', the group exclaims, even as they take up opportunities to record in nice studios in London because EMI think they are. It's a cyclical thing in the music industry – young creatives getting in the back door because the keepers of the house don't have a clue what is going on.[7]

The Saints 1973–8 were basically the creative pairing of Kuepper, guitarist and Bailey, singer. The majority of the material released from this period is credited to both, though a crucial handful of the forty or so original songs the group issued – 'Demolition Girl', 'Orstralia', 'Brisbane (Security City)', 'Everything's Fine' and others – are by Kuepper solo. His musical omnivorousness precludes a simple listing of 'influences', but some coordinates might be plotted if

---

[6]   Ingham, 'Singles', 37.

[7]   It's not uncommon to read claims that '(I'm) Stranded' was the first punk single. Such claims are based on the fact that it was released, according to various sources, in either August or September 1976, 'beating' The Damned's debut single 'New Rose' (October 1976) and Sex Pistols' 'Anarchy in the UK' (November 1976). However, as Andrew P. Street writes (The Long and Winding Way, 72): 'The reason that everyone makes the point that Australia beat England to punk is partly because we still have a massive inferiority complex when it comes to the motherland and thus overstate the importance of every tiny, meaningless victory over the Brits.' Street notes that this conveniently overlooks American artists; the Ramones' self-titled debut album was released in April 1976. In terms of independent singles that were later designated part of the continuum of mid-1970s punk rock, we might also mention Television's 'Little Johnny Jewel' and Pere Ubu's '30 Seconds Over Tokyo' (both late 1975) and Patti Smith's debut album Horses (November 1975, on major label Arista).

we pay attention. The Beatles were the group that initially made Kuepper want to play music. Six months after his parents bought him his first guitar, a Hofner Club 40, he was excited to see George Young of The Easybeats playing the same model on a TV broadcast. It was many years before he saved up and bought the Gibson SG he is seen playing with The Saints. That model was chosen because it featured on three early Kuepper LP purchases: The Who's *Live at Leeds*, The Rolling Stones' *Get Yer Ya-Yas Out* and Black Sabbath's *Paranoid*.

So far, so suburban 1970 (the year in which all three of these albums were released). It should be noted, though, that Pete Townshend of The Who and Tony Iommi of Sabbath both favour heavily overdriven guitar timbres in groups where, as the only harmonic instrument, they have a lot of space to fill. This strategy is not dissimilar to the default of punk rock, the line-up of The Saints, that of Laughing Clowns beyond the early line-ups featuring piano, and in fact nearly all of Kuepper's endeavours save for certain iterations of The Yard Goes On Forever and The Aints!. It speaks to the monolithic guitar sounds Kuepper would build for *Today Wonder* and beyond and which have been a mainstay of his concerts for the last thirty years. Speaking of Iommi and Townshend's SG tones, Kuepper says, 'the guitar could almost be there by itself, and be the band.'[8]

He sees The Saints starting in 1973 in a vacuum, where 'the sort of things that I identified with had all kind of finished' – he mentions The Velvet Underground, The MC5 and The Stooges.

---

[8]   Wilsteed, op. cit. On The Beatles and The Easybeats, 4:45–6:40. On the SG, The Who, The Rolling Stones and Black Sabbath, 15:00–17:10.

He cites Ron Asheton of the Stooges as 'a major influence' on him as a guitarist, and heard common cause between the nascent Saints and the New York Dolls' 'Frankenstein' (1973). Yet he was never one to pick up music from records. He had a brief spell playing along to B.B. King records of a certain period, not to learn B.B.'s licks or emulate his style but because the records were sparse enough for him to find a place to play in them. With respect to The Saints and punk, he says that the term was already around before the mid-1970s, applied to garage rock groups such as The Chocolate Watch Band and The Blues Magoos. It's worth noting that The Saints covered an Australian 'Sixties Punk' group on their debut album, with their version of the Missing Links' 'Wild About You'. Most of the influence of punk in Australia was of the UK variety, Kuepper says, and by the time it got to Australia, The Saints had split. Even those US touchstones such as the Stooges and The MC5 were not a focus of veneration for him as they were for, say, Radio Birdman. 'If it isn't Bo Diddley or Chuck Berry or Buddy Holly or something, I find it kind of hard to … [mimes doffing his hat].'[9]

Indeed, looking back in 2004, Kuepper offered this summary of reference points for The Saints:

> In Brisbane I was really keen to bring in as much '50s R&B and '60s stuff as possible that wasn't too mainstream. I hated most contemporary music … We weren't drawing on The Beatles or anything like that, there was a whole bunch of

---

[9]   Ibid., 21:00–27:00. Kuepper avoided the New York Dolls for a while because he hated their image, seeing them as Johnny-Come-Latelys to glam. After finally buying their debut album and particularly upon hearing 'Frankenstein', he decided, 'OK, they look like dickheads, but I love 'em!' (21:30–24:10).

stuff out of Europe – Can, Mott The Hoople, Hawkwind – that had a profound influence on me even though you'd never confuse what we were doing with any of those bands.[10]

Despite the quick evolution of The Saints across their three albums, and of Kuepper into the Laughing Clowns, parts of Kuepper's aesthetic arrived fully formed for one so young; he was twenty when The Saints recorded '(I'm) Stranded' and still only twenty-two when they split. A case in point on The Saints' debut album *(I'm) Stranded* (1977) is 'Messin' with the Kid'. At six minutes in length, it is a square-peg statement on a record generally filed under 'punk rock'. It unfolds slowly and with minimal harmonic means, just like many of the pieces on *Honey Steel's Gold*. The simple guitar melody that repeats in the track's coda performs a similar function to many instrument-played melodies throughout Kuepper's catalogue. Although co-written with Bailey, it shares with much of Kuepper's work a kind of world-weariness; a philosophical making-do with the cards dealt. 'Sometimes you get that old lost feeling. Sometimes it hits you when you're feeling down.' It is apparently a song that Kuepper values, as it has often appeared in his performances over the forty-five years since it was released. In the 2022 shows of Kuepper's with Jim White, he dedicated the song to Bailey, who had recently died.

Elsewhere on *(I'm) Stranded* we hear other signposts to future Kuepper, particularly in the mid-tempo solo composition 'Story of Love', which would not be out of place on any number of his 1980s and 1990s releases, and 'Nights In Venice': talk about bloody-mindedness! The sheer assault

---

[10]   Creswell, untitled, 9.

of this track, which closes the album with a scorched-earth aesthetic, speaks to both the monolithic guitars of The Aints' *Ascension* and Kuepper's ongoing fascination with pushing guitars to timbral extremes, whether this is through the use of volume and distortion or processing and synthesis.

The Saints' second LP, *Eternally Yours* (1978), presents a more measured, somewhat refined approach. Beyond the brass section hook of 'Know Your Product', the album was the result of more studio time rather than a wholescale reimagining of the group. Kuepper says

> the *(I'm) Stranded* album is a summation of the Brisbane era
> … that's the end of Chapter 1. Now we actually move into the
> outside world, and we can use multitrack recording studios,
> we can actually spend more than two days in a studio. We
> can even do things like hire brass sections if we want to.

The album is split between the fast and raw shapes of the debut, heard on tracks such as 'Lost and Found', 'Run Down' and 'Misunderstood', acoustic guitar-driven mid-pacers such as 'Memories Are Made of This', 'A Minor Aversion' and 'Untitled', and points between like 'No, Your Product', 'This Perfect Day' and 'Orstralia', which fuse the energy of the debut with a new sophistication. Then there's 'Know Your Product'. The track that kicked off *Eternally Yours* is a classic slice of snarling rhythm and blues, an Australian rock standard, and a hit that never was. I remember the impact it made at the time, in Australia at least through Double J radio in Sydney and *Countdown* on national TV, despite its lack of chart success.[11] Lyrically updating the

---

[11] This website, which contains a detailed chronology of The Saints' career, confirms my memory of seeing the film clip of 'Know Your Product' on *Countdown*, though no specific date is given beyond 1978. https://www.fromthearchives.org/ts/chronology.html, accessed 25 July 2022.

Rolling Stones' 'Satisfaction', and equalling that band's best work, the other plot points of The Saints' narrative suggest that this track must have been released at the point at which EMI had lost promotional interest in the group. A crucial factor was that in early 1978, the fashion-conscious British music scene probably wasn't ready for 'punk rock' with horns.

The real leap was made with the third LP, the final one of the Kuepper/Bailey collaboration, *Prehistoric Sounds* (also 1978). Though a brass section had been used on *Eternally Yours*, it was further integrated, and integral to a broader range of grooves than the group had attempted before. Notable was the swing of 'Swing For The Crime' and 'Crazy Googenheimer Blues', the rock waltz of 'All Times Through Paradise', the rhythm and blues strut of 'Everything's Fine'. The darker moods of 'All Times' and 'Brisbane (Security City)' set the course for the more torrid emotional terrain of the Clowns. The important melodic lines given to brass on 'Swing for the Crime' and 'Everything's Fine' again point to the Clowns, as does the brief alto sax solo on 'All Times'.

The release of *Prehistoric Sounds* was bungled, even undermined in effect, by EMI's lack of attention. The group included covers of Otis Redding's 'Security' and Aretha Franklin's 'Save Me' on the album. Though the former, at least, was at the record company's suggestion, it was a song that The Saints had been playing with. In fact, another example of that Kuepper/Saints bloody-mindedness was the tour, with a brass section, that The Saints did on the back of *Eternally Yours*. It confounded punk-minded audiences. EMI released 'Security' as *Prehistoric Sounds*' only single; one can only imagine what might have happened if they'd gone for the catchy and assured 'Everything's Fine'.

In fact, that horn-festooned tour was pretty much the end of The Saints. Bailey had quit, and had to be coaxed back to record the final instalment of the group's three-record deal with EMI. Kuepper had been writing and wasn't about to let the opportunity slip. After *Prehistoric Sounds*, it looked for a moment as though E.G. Records (home of Roxy Music, Brian Eno and King Crimson) might be interested in The Saints. The two songwriters met: Kuepper offered 'The Laughing Clowns', Bailey offered 'On The Waterfront'.[12] 'I wasn't particularly crazy about what he'd written', remembers Kuepper. 'I thought it was kind of a pub rock tune, and he thought that what I'd written was some pretentious piece of delusional nonsense.'[13] They kept the fact that the band was no longer an entity quiet until EMI released the album. After the split, Kuepper spent the rest of 1978 in England, wondering whether that was the end of his music career.

*

Kuepper makes for an interesting case study for the categorization of music. It's his prerogative to reject any categories in which we might place any of his music, but it does make sense to think of The Saints in terms of punk, and Laughing Clowns in terms of post-punk. What I think irks Kuepper about The Saints being thought of as a punk band is the idea of following a trend. As he is famously quoted as saying:

> The Saints have been constantly lumped in with the Sex
> Pistols and The Clash and all that, and we really had nothing

---

[12] Thompson, '1975 Ed Kuepper's Valeno Guitar'. Though Kuepper's presentation of 'The Laughing Clowns' at this meeting is well documented, this is the only source I have found that identifies 'On the Waterfront' as the song Bailey brought to this meeting.

[13] McFarlane, 'Ed Kuepper | Long Play Series', 1:07:51–1:08:07.

to do with it. The band was a full thing by 1974. Two and a half years later, this incredibly fashionable movement comes along, only an arsehole would have associated himself with that.[14]

But of course, this depends on how we define punk, or punk rock. Though each of the pivotal punk groups has their own mix of influences – (the) Sex Pistols and (the) Ramones are very different from each other, despite supplying the most prominent archetypes – what they share is a reduction of pop/rock to the basic rudiments of guitar-bass-drums-vocal. They eschewed commonly accepted notions of musical competency, while continuing to embrace fairly standardized song forms. The important caveat is that The Saints made one punk rock album, ([I'm] Stranded), a second that might be thought of more straightforwardly as a rock album as it pivots from punk rock towards other options (Eternally Yours,) and a third that is one of the first post-punk albums (Prehistoric Sounds).

Why do I describe Prehistoric Sounds and the output of Laughing Clowns as post-punk? Simon Reynolds provides a succinct definition, suggesting it applies to artists 'who saw 1977 not as a return to raw rock 'n' roll but the chance to make a break with tradition, and who defined punk as an imperative to constant change'.[15] I am not suggesting that Kuepper formed The Saints with Bailey with an agenda of constant change in mind; we can surmise that each was interested in writing original songs, and in pursuing opportunities making rock music. But we do know that it was Kuepper that pushed The Saints, with his songwriting and arrangements,

---

14 Walker, Stranded, 72.
15 Reynolds, Rip It Up, xvii.

into incorporating brass on their second and third albums. He convinced Bailey to persevere with the third album even though the direction of the record was not Bailey's vision. Kuepper was also the one who took that leap into the void with Laughing Clowns, creating elusive and confronting compositions and recordings that strove to take rock music somewhere new. Post-punk is a convenient catch-all for a very disparate bunch of artists: Joy Division, The Birthday Party, Siouxsie and the Banshees, Tuxedomoon, Magazine, Pere Ubu, The Slits, The Fall … Laughing Clowns. What they have in common is some kernel of disenfranchisement by the state of rock music in the mid-1970s that led to a singular expression of creativity related to, but (this part is important) not bound by traditions of rock music.

It also makes sense to describe Kuepper as a singer-songwriter, particularly from the start of his solo career in 1985. And, although the late 1960s/early 1970s formation of the singer-songwriter is significant to him, as evidenced in his covers of songs by artists such as Tim Hardin and Gordon Lightfoot, I use the term in the context of Kuepper as a mode of operation rather than a genre category. Kuepper writes, records and sings his own music, which tends to be song-based. *Honey Steel's Gold* is a perfect representation of the ways in which Kuepper is *sui generis*. He's certainly not bound to the early 1970s definition of the singer-songwriter, no more than he is bound to the searing guitar tone of the likes of Ron Asheton or the post-war blues of John Lee Hooker, or the late 1960s Australian rock of The Loved Ones. All, and much more, are part of the mix for a musician who is also a record fiend; whose discoveries of jazz as a resident in London in the late 1970s impacted upon the direction of Laughing Clowns; who posted to Facebook a selection of old cassettes he and Jim White were apparently enjoying on tour in 2022.[16]

Laughing Clowns – The Only One That Knows

It's such a cliché to describe a musical artist as original, unique, singular. But one listen to the recorded output of Laughing Clowns and you know that what might seem like hyperbole in other contexts is justified here. OK, in the broader context of post-punk, there were other groups that incorporated brass and the influence of jazz into their stew. Probably the best of these is Rip, Rig and Panic, named after an album by Roland Kirk and at times offering an exhilarating collision between dub, jazz and funk, studio techniques and live performance, shot through with a punk sense of chaos. But to put Laughing Clowns in a category with them (beyond the broad catch-all of post-punk) would be misguided. Unlike Rip, Rig and Panic, Laughing Clowns are a rock band, based on songs. This might seem a churlish distinction, but jazz is such

---

[16] Compilations of Patsy Cline and Buddy Holly, *Beatles for Sale*, Neil Diamond's *Moods*, Status Quo's *Dog of Two Head*, David Bowie's *Man Who Sold the World*, The Kinks' *Preservation Act 1*, Black Sabbath's *Sabbath Bloody Sabbath*, Townshend and Laine's *Rough Mix*, Thunderclap Newman's *Hollywood Dream* and Bobbie Gentry's *Ode to Billy Joe*. Posted to the Ed Kuepper Music Facebook page on 5 May 2022, Kuepper describes this selection of tapes as being 'from the days when you could go camping on the beach for free'.

an abused word, so easily bandied about in the context of rock reviews, that any group with a saxophone is in danger of being so-branded. As Kuepper says, 'The Clowns, for all their reputation for being a free-form jazz ensemble, were actually very heavily arranged, with little moments of improvisation.'

With Laughing Clowns (and earlier, The Saints), Ed conceptualized a new way forward for his music oblivious to, and if anything slightly ahead of developments in the northern hemisphere: they formed in early 1979, played their first shows in August of that year, and finally unravelled at the start of 1985.[17] Essentially, rather than free jazz, jazz rock or any of the other inadequate descriptions thrown at them, the Clowns created rock music spun into unusual shapes, somewhat informed by elements of jazz. In the period leading up to the recording of *Prehistoric Sounds*, Kuepper

> discovered a whole range of music, or at least looked into it deeper – avant garde jazz, '60s Archie Shepp, Sun Ra, all that stuff. I'd had little glimpses of it but it started to make more sense to me when I was in England for some reason. I also started to go back to country music and bluegrass, which I'd heard a bit as a kid.[18]

At the time of the release of the Laughing Clowns box set, Kuepper said that the two primary influences on the group

---

[17] David Nichols suggests some contexts for what Laughing Clowns was doing: he describes London's Essential Logic and New York City's Contortions, contemporary to the Clowns, as 'kindred spirits', and Sydney-based groups Out of Nowhere, Wildlife Documentaries and Upside Down House, each of which included Kuepper's former bandmates in either the Clowns or The Saints, as 'shar[ing] some of the same reference points'. See Nichols, *Dig*, 428, 431.

[18] Creswell, untitled, 17.

when they were starting were Shepp and a Tony Bennett album called *The Beat of My Heart*.[19] Kuepper's liner notes in the box set, where he gives a pithy paragraph on each track, include references to a lot of jazz on the freer end of the spectrum. Ornette Coleman, Roland Kirk, John Coltrane, Sun Ra and Pharaoh Sanders all get mentions, but so do the blues and rhythm and blues of Slim Harpo, Lee Dorsey, and Bo Diddley, as well as spaghetti westerns, surf music, cartoon themes, Kraftwerk, Jimmy Webb's work with Richard Harris ... and Status Quo, in the sense of his imagining that the Quo should have covered the Clowns track 'In Front of Your Eyes'.[20]

This list of reference points is a kind of cul-de-sac. Such is Kuepper's wide frame of reference, and the nature of his creative processes that synthesize the input, that these interests remain obscure until Kuepper points to them. They function as a barely perceived and incomplete reservoir of sounds drawn on unconsciously. Listening to music from throughout Kuepper's career I think about the relationship between artistic statements and dreams. Unless based on a very conscious instrumentality, acts of creativity are to some degree attempts to communicate with those parts of ourselves that are below the surface. Just as our dreams jumble recent experiences and interactions with primal fears, ongoing trauma and ambitions for the future, so does the artist, unconsciously, dip their ladle into a kind of residual sensory soup.[21]

---

[19] Pottinger, untitled.

[20] Kuepper, 'Blow by blow'.

[21] Although I don't believe he used the exact analogies of dipping a ladle, or sensory soup, this idea was introduced to me by Robyn Hitchcock when I interviewed him in 1993. The piece was never published, and damned if I can find it.

This sensory soup is not limited to music; as I will discuss in more detail further on, Kuepper refers to films, and the idea of writing soundtracks as important to his songwriting, especially during the Laughing Clowns period. 'Theme from "Mad Flies, Mad Flies"' was intended for a never-completed animation; the title of 'Knife in the Head' was 'lifted from a German film that was around at the time'; 'The Flypaper' 'evolved out of my liking for spaghetti westerns'; of 'Come One Come All', Kuepper writes 'I wanted a soundtrack, not for voodoo ritual, but some kind of sinister situation', and so on.[22]

Those of us obsessed with our record collections (guilty as charged) or otherwise immersed in the churn of popular music can get very stuck on the idea of 'musical influences' (see above). Beyond music, film and other cultural artefacts, there are the details of everyday living, as each of us finds them: the cups and saucers, the rooms and gardens, the landscapes, cityscapes and suburb-scapes that coalesce as the background radiation of our consciousnesses. A reserve in Kuepper's home suburb of Oxley, Brisbane, was officially named Ed Kuepper Park in 2018, and Kuepper wrote on the Laughing Clowns Facebook page that it is 'right near where some of the stories from the reflective [Laughing Clowns album] *Law of Nature* took place'.[23] We'll see later that a private cartography is also discernible in aspects of *Honey Steel's Gold*.

*

In writing a book about an artist with such an imposing discography, and such a powerful sense of dogged artistic

---

[22] All these bits of commentary, Kuepper, op. cit.

[23] Kuepper, uncredited, https://www.facebook.com/laughingclowns/, post of 17 February 2018. I have added the italics to the album title.

progression, it is easy to fall into the trap of giving all credit to the individual. In the case of Laughing Clowns, we would do well to acknowledge the contribution of significant others. Eminent Australian music critic Clinton Walker, a confidant of Kuepper's from their initial interactions in the tiny Brisbane coterie that formed around The Saints, writes that '[p]eople used to go and see the Laughing Clowns just to watch Jeffrey Wegener in action'.[24] Anyone familiar with the recordings of Laughing Clowns will know the sound and *feel* of Wegener's drumming, will have absorbed it as the skittering pulse of this inimitable music. Wegener was the only member of the group that stayed constant alongside Kuepper. Walker goes on:

> Kuepper's natural reserve found release as a foil to Jeffrey in the Laughing Clowns. I can vividly remember watching the Clowns. The band would be blazing and a small smile would come across Kuepper's face, just the corner of his mouth upturning, as if in acknowledgement of Jeffrey. And Jeffrey would just keep driving harder.[25]

But we might also attribute this relationship, essential to the identity of the band, to Kuepper's uncanny, seldom remarked upon abilities as a bandleader. If the early horn players in the Clowns contributed an essential service by playing his melodic lines and improvising in a free and discordant manner when required, in Louise Elliott, the tenor saxophonist who joined the group in 1981, Kuepper found a true comrade. As well as fulfilling the capacities already described, Elliott is a superlative soloist, such as on the justly celebrated second half of 'Eternally Yours', and possesses a rich and wily timbre that is all her own.

---

24 Walker, *Stranded*, 121.

25 Ibid., 122.

Like a jazz player, she develops motivic ideas and has an intuitive sense of how to blend notes and noises for maximum impact. As well as expressing her own individuality, her solos at times seem to channel the raw emotional material that comprises the compositions. Although ultimately Laughing Clowns is defined by Kuepper's exploratory songwriting, and the thinking he applied to arranging music that exploded the existing paradigms of rock – to the extent that audiences and critics of the time often seemed to fail to recognize that the Clowns *is* a rock band – it is Wegener and Elliott who for years put the flesh on the bone, animated the songs' carefully constructed skeletons and made them dance with such character.[26]

It seems to me that as much as it is a crucial chapter of Kuepper's ongoing story as a performer, composer and recording artist, the period of Laughing Clowns was where he honed that bandleader's ability to choose musicians appropriate to his projects. For the *Law of Nature* album, he got pianist Chris Abrahams on board; Abrahams would also contribute to Kuepper's second solo album *Rooms of the Magnificent*, and, as we've already seen, help to define the soundscape of *Honey Steel's Gold* by playing the first notes we hear on the album. Abrahams is a perfect collaborator for Kuepper in that he is a one-off, at the time of *Law of Nature* swimming in the world of jazz of The Benders but really a protean improvising musician

---

[26] I've drawn this conclusion from my engagement with Laughing Clowns' records, but Peter Walsh, having just finished up playing bass for the group at the time, expressed similar thoughts in 1984: 'Both Jeffrey and LouLou [Elliott] are fairly assertive because it's their future. And they drive the material. The guts of the material's there, and the signature is a shared one.' Quoted in Nichols, *Dig*, 430.

beyond genre. With Lloyd Swanton on double bass and Tony Buck on drums, Abrahams would form the internationally celebrated, inimitable improvising trio The Necks. Similarly, Kuepper worked for a decade with drummer Mark Dawson, first the propulsive force of The Yard Goes On Forever, then the co-forger of *Today Wonder* and empathetic mainstay of Kuepper's prolific output of the first half of the 1990s. We might make similar observations of Kuepper's musical connections with pianist Alister Spence and drummer Jim White.

Though their discography suggests nine different line-ups of the band, Kuepper sees the Clowns as having three distinct stages. The initial line-up of four swelled to five and then six; over this period the group staked their territory with three astonishing EPs: *Laughing Clowns* (1980); *Sometimes the Fire Dance* (1981) and *3* (1981), compiling the second and third releases as *Reign of Blood, Throne of Terror* (1981). This is the only phase of the band in which piano is integral; where a pianist (Dan Wallace-Crabbe) is an ongoing member of the band.[27] The piano and squawking saxophone and trumpet connoted free jazz for many, but as Kuepper asserts any chaos was tightly controlled. Possibly the most enduring tunes from this era are the haunting, funereal 'Collapse Board', a staple of Kuepper's setlist through to the time of writing, and 'Sometimes', an upbeat pop song driven by an indelible sax melody that at the end of the song becomes a sung refrain (*craft*, my friends! It was the chorus all along!). Incongruously, the lyrics concern the grim scenario of the death of someone that 'didn't rate a mention'.

---

[27] The caveat here is that Alister Spence was part of the line-up for the Laughing Clowns reformation gigs in 2009.

The next stage of the group saw, after the depletion of the ranks, the arrivals of both Louise Elliott and Leslie 'Biff' Millar. Millar is the only double bassist, rather than bass guitarist to have been a member of the Clowns, and his fluid, breathtaking lines again made something of a connection to the idea of jazz. They're heard to best effect on the EP *Everything That Flies* (1983), one of the most sympathetic recordings of any line-up of the group and a personal favourite of Kuepper's. This had been preceded by the group's first full-length album *Mr Uddich-Smuddich Goes to Town* (1982). Although Kuepper was not quite satisfied with this record, as usual it features strong writing as well as a bona fide indie hit. The aforementioned 'Theme from "Mad Flies, Mad Flies"' was released as a single, and its three-ring flea-circus theme and buzzing double bass produce a high-wire thrill that's also a novel piece of pop.

The final phase of the Clowns saw a deliberate streamlining take place. Kuepper felt that the improvisation aspect of the group had gone too far with *Uddich-Smuddich* and the following tour; the correction started with the *Everything That Flies* EP and was consolidated with the departure of Millar, leaving a core of Kuepper, Elliott and Wegener, bolstered by Peter Walsh of The Apartments on bass, and then Paul Smith, who would kick on to anchor The Yard with Mark Dawson. The recorded output became more concentrated in this era – two full-length albums rather than the briefer reports of EPs that had dominated thus far.

Law of Nature (1984) still features some of the experimental elements of the Laughing Clowns repertoire of yore – wrong-footing time-changes in 'Written in Exile' and 'As Your Bridges Burn Behind You', no lack of flattened-fifth harmonies, but also a keener focus on the vocal and more concise song forms. Although it spins out to an extended coda that features Elliott, 'Eternally Yours' was a signpost to Kuepper's solo work. A single chord progression sustains the entire piece, and both the saxophone melody and the vocal melody with which it alternates are simple and memorable. The music has an air of determination through the acceptance of some difficult truth; perhaps ultimately a sense of triumph indicated by Elliott's irrepressible solo. It has justly become one of the most celebrated songs of Kuepper's career.

Ghosts of an Ideal Wife (1985) was begun as the band was falling apart and completed by Kuepper in the aftermath, taking several months to see the light of day. It features a couple of older songs – 'Winter's Way' was written in 1975, and 'The Only One That Knows', a proper epic like those found on earlier Clowns records, unsurprisingly dates from then – and again, several songs feature disruptive tempo or time signature changes. But there are also more straightforward songs such as 'No Words of Honour', 'New Bully in Town' and the title track that make for something of a stylistic crossover with Kuepper's debut solo album *Electrical Storm* (also 1985). In fact, both 'Bully' and 'Ghosts' would be rerecorded by The Yard, and 'Bully' was a staple of early solo/Yard shows. While epic forms and songs that shift gear in terms of tempo and feel are strategies that return throughout Kuepper's discography, he would never really return to the extended and at times discordant harmony of the Clowns years; at least not in his song-based material.

Ed Kuepper Park Is Melting in the Dark (the Early Solo Years)

Richard Harris's 'MacArthur Park', a huge international hit in 1968, is now very much an acquired taste. The seven-and-a-half minutes of drama, with an overblown arrangement including orchestra and harpsichord, would be enough to put many people off, without Harris's dramatic enunciation of the psychedelic-prismed lyric. OK, it's a classic of sorts; the song had the longevity to be a global smash in disco garb for Donna Summer a decade later. It was composed by Jimmy Webb, also responsible for Glen Campbell perennials 'Galveston', 'Wichita Lineman' and 'By the Time I Get to Phoenix', as well as The Fifth Dimension's 'Up, Up and Away'. 'MacArthur Park' is on *A Tramp Shining*, the first of two albums Harris would record with Webb as producer and sole composer. The second is called *The Yard Went on Forever*.

We've seen that Kuepper saw fit to mention the Harris/Webb collaboration in reference to Laughing Clowns; specifically it was to 'The Only One That Knows', a song that lurches through several sections, just like 'MacArthur Park' or indeed 'The Yard Went On Forever'. Calling his early solo career group The Yard Goes On Forever was, perhaps, a sincere tip of the lid to those Harris/Webb recordings, but equally it might have been just another absurd gesture. After all, Black Sabbath were pretty fond of a multi-sectioned epic too, and Sabbath's Tony Iommi has been mentioned by Kuepper as a foundational influence on his guitar playing. I look forward to Ed Kuepper and the Masters of Reality.

The Yard was another group that went through a number of line-ups, but existed in one shape or other from 1986 to 1989. However, Kuepper's first solo album *Electrical Storm* predates the Yard. It wiped the slate clean, an album of mostly bright pop songs roughly recorded and driven by acoustic guitar. Though they had been part of the mix of his music since the start, folk and blues elements were laid bare on this record in a way that set the scene for the solo records that followed. The title track and 'Car Headlights' are tracks Kuepper has repeatedly returned to both in live sets and in recorded remakes.

Rooms of the Magnificent (1986) followed, many tracks continuing in a similar direction but with an expanded lineup. Horns were reintroduced and the record benefitted from fuller production. The first single from the album, 'Also Sprach the King of Eurodisco' was equal parts peculiar and compelling. It lopes along like a kind of country-and-western infused disco, with Kuepper's trademark melodic hooks rolling out one after the other – first on guitar, then brass, then female vocals. None of these are the vocal melodies of the verse or chorus. Kuepper really is, as much as any of his other attributes, a font of melodies. They just seem to pour out of him – this track is a masterclass in melody writing and arrangement.

Just as *Today Wonder* was a fresh beginning which *Honey Steel's Gold* then built on, we might see the relationship between *Electrical Storm* and *Rooms of the Magnificent* in the same way. Going further, each of these 'restart' albums was a reaction to something of a creative impasse. I am not suggesting that Kuepper was running out of ideas before either *Electrical Storm* or *Today Wonder*, but that each was prompted by a desire to do something entirely different to what had come directly before them. Both albums were achieved by a jettisoning of personnel – in fact, the breaking up of a long-standing group – and a returning to principles of minimalism, which seems to be Kuepper's surest way to reset. With *Electrical Storm*, Kuepper was responding to close to six years of composing for, and looking after a group called Laughing Clowns. In the case of *Today Wonder*, he closed the door on The Yard, and retreated from what in hindsight he might have seen as a Faustian pact with industry standards: namely, his third solo album *Everybody's Got To* (1988).

As a fan at the time, I loved Kuepper's first two solo records, but couldn't come at *Everybody's Got To*. Some thirty-five years on, the stadium snare drum and synth horns are only minor crimes against taste rather than the barrier they once were. Kuepper maintains that it is a strong set of songs, but that in the hermetic studio environment of 1988 pushing against the default synthetic sound was difficult, even for someone as hard-headed as himself.

> It's one of those sonic things. It's just too much SSL desks and Eighties reverbs, which I was fighting against, but didn't fight against strongly enough … Even if you tempered that a little bit, and you thought 'that's much better', in actual fact it should have been expelled completely … The band was really good, really tight, it just needed someone recording us like the Rolling Stones would have been recorded or something.

Of course, it's not a matter of the use of reverb – *Today Wonder* and *Honey Steel's Gold* are drunk on the stuff. At the risk of getting Marxist, it was a matter of Kuepper seizing back the means of production. It was finding studio engineers on the same page, not part of the major label hubris in which *Everybody's Got To* was made. I don't mean to invoke a major/indie dichotomy – without doubt, there can be independent label hubris as well. But from this point onwards Kuepper was careful to maintain artistic and aesthetic control. It helped that it was at this point that Kuepper found, finally, studio people who were sympathetic to the work he wanted to make. His relationship with Electric Avenue Studios, (Sydney, Australia) and engineers Adam Chapman and Phil Punch, helped to make possible the incredible flow of records he made in the first half of the 1990s. We'll pick this up in a later chapter, but for now, here is Kuepper outlining his guiding aesthetic to Clinton

Walker in the mid-1990s. It sums up a lot of what makes *Honey Steel's Gold* the alluring work that it is:

> I actually like that looseness or that slightly unpredictable feeling when you're not pounding something to death, basically. That's what I like in music. I hate slick production … I'm becoming more and more interested in the texture of sound … I've sort of got to the point where acoustic music for me is basically … you know, that's where all emotion and all power lies … It's got atmosphere, it's got mystique, it's got emotion, it's got energy, intimacy …[28]

[28]   Walker, op. cit., 404.

7   Honey Steel's Gold

If *Honey Steel's Gold* is a kind of fulcrum of Kuepper's career, the title track is the fulcrum of the album; the halfway point, the beginning of side two on the vinyl edition, a steady-as-she-goes ride into some distant horizon.

The track delivers the quintessential take on Kuepper's minimalism. It throbs on a single chord for much of its length, breaking every now and then for a three-chord turnaround. (While this is true, it is a typically inadequate use of words to describe music). This inexorable rhythm, contentedly unchanging with a bright-eyed major key melody floating above it, is rather Neu!-like; 'Honey Steel's Gold' is no less magisterial than Neu! slow-burners such as 'Seeland'.[1] But it has its own bluesy swagger. Kuepper's unhurried jamming leads into the tune's recurring melody. It's as if he's engaged

---

[1]   The Düsseldorf duo of the early mid-1970s made some of the sounds most associated with what became known as krautrock, a kind of catch-all term used to describe a wave of progressive German bands from the period of the late 1960s to the mid-1970s, most notably Can, Neu!, Faust, Tangerine Dream, Cluster, Harmonia and early Kraftwerk. At their most energetic, Neu! were proto-punk, but their most influential work unfolds at a stately pace with little appetite for harmonic changes. This approach can be heard in post-punk artists such as Joy Division, New Order and some Sonic Youth; and in post-rock artists such as Stereolab and Tortoise. Mark Dawson cites a krautrock influence on his approach to the drumming on this album (though Can was the group that came to mind for him rather than Neu!), and with material like 'Honey Steel's Gold' it is easy to hear why.

in a casual conversation, lingering on the details in a way that keeps the listener hanging on the next part of the story.

In what is typical for Kuepper, virtuosity has no place here in terms of the guitar playing. It is sensual; it is the slow hand[2] of a lover extending the pleasure. It's the creation of atmosphere that won't be compromised by showboating. Also, and again a signature of Kuepper's work, the most indelible melodic hooks are given to an instrument (here the guitar) rather than the vocal.

The sleight-of-hand here is structural. The three-chord turnaround is a chorus of sorts, though there's no singing. The single-chord chug has three iterations that all flow seamlessly into each other – Ed soloing (slowly), Ed playing that sweet major key guitar melody, and Ed singing the only words in the piece: 'Well I don't know, but I been told/The Nazis done stole Honey Steel's gold.' Somehow, this combination of elements means that as listeners we're in a blissfully static space (like the sun shining on your back on a winter's day) but we don't quite know where we are. We never quite know when the improvised phrases will give way to the sweet tune. The 'chorus' melody/chord progression tends to blindside us after we've been bobbing along on a single chord for quite a stretch … and yet it's all of a mood, just enough variation and no more.

The structural, temporal (stately pace) and timbral approach (a painter's colour chart of guitar shades made royal with reverb) of 'Honey Steel's Gold' connects with various aspects of the rest of the album. Two of the three tracks we've heard so far have been epics, and though only five-and-a-half minutes, 'Honey Steel's Gold' also has an epic feel. After it, we have

---

[2]   If you must read an intertextual reference into that idea, could we go for the Pointer Sisters rather than Eric Clapton? Thanks.

the home stretch. 'The Way I Made You Feel' is next, similarly unhurried, then the two most pop song-ish tracks at positions six and seven ('Not Too Soon' and 'Closer [But Disguised]') before a dissolve to pure texture in 'Summerfield' finishes the record. It's almost as if the quasi-ambient approach of 'King of Vice', 'Friday's Blue Cheer/Libertines of Oxley' and 'Honey Steel's Gold' prolong that structural gambit mentioned in Chapter 1 – the withholding of gratification, or of the release of tension – if we think of the album as a suite. That is, although Kuepper's distinctive melodies are irrepressible, and key to every track on the album, the sugar-hits of pure pop are doled out very gradually. Track two, 'Everything I've Got Belongs to You' is a singalong to be sure, but by the time we get to 'The Way I Made You Feel', the second more conventional song composition in the tracklisting, we are nearly half an hour into the album. A kind of tension is created through the withholding of straightforward songs in what is ostensibly a rock album. We meet the composer on his own terms; we eat the main meal before we get the dessert.

This is not to deny that there is a kind of instant gratification to the pure beauty of Chris Abrahams's rolling out of the piano melody of 'King of Vice'; sheer pleasure in the shimmering guitar textures and bodacious Bo Diddley groove of 'Friday's Blue Cheer/Libertines of Oxley' and the meditative stroll of 'Honey Steel's Gold'. Despite tracks of eight and ten minutes' duration, there's not a second wasted on this album. It's as if Kuepper presaged the slow food movement with a slow rock movement. And it's not that the music is slow (though it is blissfully unhurried), so much as the album is structured for sustained pleasure.

*

The Return of the Red Herring – the next instalment in an Ed K. series. The title of this tune (and album), its meagre but evocative lyric, and a cryptic inscription in the lyric sheet give way to layers of intrigue. You might want to get a drink, I could be here for a while …

1. Is there a Honey Steel? For my sins, I searched the Internet until I found reference to Phyllis 'Grandma Honey' Steel. She was born in 1939, died in 1998, and is buried in Wildwood Cemetery, Polk, Florida. I have no reason to believe that she had any gold, or if she did, that the Nazis stole it.

2. 'I don't know, but I've been told' … As a person of a certain age with shelves full of vinyl, I have antennae trained for certain types of intertextual references. It's very difficult to turn off, an element of what I call Discographical Tourette's – the tendency to spout trivia about records given the slightest opening. So 'I don't know, but I've been told' hits me right in the *Led Zeppelin IV* – 'Black Dog' to be precise. I had vaguely thought that it was probably swiped from an old blues song, as so much of Zeppelin's gear is. But actually, no. Or perhaps sort-of. The line is a classic trope of the US military cadence, or 'jody call'. I don't watch a lot of war movies, but think of those scenes where a drill sergeant barks semi-sung lines to marching troops, who bellow them back in rhythm to their uniformed, stomping feet. Who knows where it came from originally?

   So … *Led Zep IV* was released in 1971. The Vietnam War was still grinding on, and a prime target for the disaffection of the counter-culture. It stands to reason that Zeppelin incorporated a military cadence into their rock music, disguising it as a blues trope, as a provocation. The desired response would be 'who are these long-haired Limey peaceniks using our good honest army lines?' Though I don't claim to be an authority on Led Zeppelin, I can't recall anyone making this connection. Yet, how cool is that, a little bomb embedded in a song that's waited fifty years to go off in my head?

Ed Kuepper turned fifteen at the end of 1970. Throughout his career he has repeatedly referenced music from the late 1960s and early 1970s – the period of his teenage years. This is unremarkable; it's common wisdom that we're imprinted with the music of our teenage years in a way that music heard later can never shake. It's the period when we consciously differentiate ourselves from our parents and are insatiable for signs of what the world really is, outside of our domestic and educational pods (unless, as seems increasingly the case in the age of social media, this period is one of an anxiety that keeps us fixed to the small screens that in no small way induced the social phobias to begin with). It's when we most keenly look around for role models. So it's more than likely that Kuepper is giving a cheeky wink to Page, Plant, Jones and Bonham here.

But wait a minute – the song mentions the Nazis! A quotation of a military trope in a lyric that references the most notorious war criminals in recent history. That might just be a coincidence, I suppose … but at this point we cannot completely dismiss Kuepper's German heritage. Although the lyric is obscure, we can't help but ask why a songwriter of this background would include this reference. A dear friend and ex-flatmate of mine of German extraction once told me of his feelings of guilt for the atrocities of the Second World War, despite the fact of being born in the late 1970s. Though equating 'Honey Steel's Gold' with guilt in the songwriter would be presumptuous, it is not too far-fetched to think that there might be a residue of inherited trauma coursing through it.[3]

3. Underneath the lyrics for this song in the CD booklet, in smaller handwriting (the lyrics appear to all be in the Kuepper hand) is the legend 'CCR vs 3rd Reich'. I don't hear any musical reference to Creedence Clearwater Revival in the track, unless we get quite conceptual and speculate that their 'Susie Q' (1968) is also an inexorable chug of minimal musical means. Tenuous at best. But we can say that Creedence hit that Kuepper-teen sweet spot as a group that ruled the world's singles charts from 1968 to 1971. The phrase amuses Kuepper enough that he retooled it on his

---

[3] My thanks to Jon Stratton for his suggestion that I consider this aspect of the song further. Stratton also suggested to me that the line 'I don't know but I've been told' comes from Bob Dylan's 'I Shall Be Free #10' (1964), where the thought is completed with 'The streets of heaven are lined with gold'. Dylan also used a variant of this line in his arrangement of the African-American spiritual 'Gospel Plow' (1962). Given that these are relatively obscure Dylan recordings, and Kuepper's abiding references to a popular music ground zero of 1970, I think it much more likely the Led Zeppelin recording is the immediate source. Intriguingly, the couplet 'I don't know but I've been told/The streets of heaven are *paved* with gold' is present in Simon and Garfunkel's 'You Can Tell the World' (1964), and the version of this song by The Seekers (1965), but not the arrangement these versions seem to stem from by The Tarriers (1960). The source of all these folk revival-era recordings would seem to be 'Then He Brought Joy to My Soul' by the Taskiana Four (1926). Finally, the couplet is also present in a recording by The Partridge Family, 'Love Must Be the Answer' (1972). With thanks to Google, Wikipedia, YouTube and secondhandsongs.com.

1995 album *A King in the Kindness Room* as 'They Call Me Mr. Sexy (Love Theme from C.C.R. versus the 3rd Reich)'.

But again, maybe there's more to this than an in-joke. The relevance of Kuepper's origins in Brisbane and birth in Germany are not at the forefront of this study – I perceive Kuepper as an Australian artist first and foremost, and *Honey Steel's Gold* as an Australian record. But I keep coming back to the idea of the corrupt Joh Bjelke-Petersen government, and how any kind of youth culture of that time can only be seen as being in opposition or defiance to it. Bjelke-Petersen was premier of Queensland from 1968 to 1987, and his authoritarian regime must have cast a shadow over anyone, such as Kuepper, who spent their teenage years and young adulthood in Brisbane.

'The Nazis done stole Honey Steel's gold'. Putting aside the provenance of the name Honey Steel, we might receive it as a stand-in for the people of Queensland whose finances were ransacked by a rapacious premier and ministry, or more specifically the youth of Brisbane trying to create their own culture.[4] The stories of the harassment, violence towards, and spurious imprisonment of participants in the fledgling music scenes of mid to late 1970s Brisbane are legion.[5] We might think of the far-right police state mentality of Bjelke-Petersen's Queensland (the 'Nazis') attempting to obliterate anything that enabled young people to congregate around music – stealing their gold. If positing that The Saints are the band in the construction 'CCR vs the 3rd Reich' is a bit too reductionist, we might see the grass-roots, goodtime rock

---

[4]   See Bongiorno, *The Eighties*, 267–71 for a precis of the corruption of the Bjelke-Petersen government.
[5]   For a sample of these horrific stories, see Stafford, *Pig City*, 94–112.

and roll of Creedence Clearwater Revival as emblematic of the positive energy of Brisbane's mid-1970s music scene.[6]

4. Yes, I could just ask Kuepper about the resonances he intended with these titles and lyrics. But where's the fun in that? In any case, I don't believe in right or wrong answers to this kind of thing. The power of any creative work is the evocative spell it casts on us – the possibilities it opens to us. As I mentioned earlier, the mission here is to engage with the spell, the spectrum, the splendour of this record, not to try to tie it down in a kind of questionnaire. It doesn't even matter if you think I'm way off-base with the above speculations. If nothing else they demonstrate the deep places one can go if one is prepared to wonder, and wander. The 'meaning' of any art is not to be dictated by the maker, or found in any one interpretation. It exists in a luminous, ever-becoming space between the two.[7]

*

At the risk of spoiling the party, there is something of a correct answer, which I place here at the end of the discussion

---

[6] In an interview in 2021 (Kendall, 'Meet'), Kuepper said that the Brisbane The Saints developed in was 'a fairly big country town', and that 'The Saints left Queensland before the overbearing police state stuff started happening – I mean Bjelke-Petersen was there, but he wasn't as powerful – that happened more in the late seventies going into the late eighties [sic] … I think sometimes the negatives get a little romanticised'. But let's not let the artist's perspective get in the way of good speculation.

[7] Uncanny. Four days after writing this I found the following in Will Brooker's *Why Bowie Matters*: 'Our interpretations can go beyond Bowie's original intentions. These aren't competitive quizzes … they are maps, where we can wander (and wonder) alone, or examine the signposts and see where they take us' (87).

purposefully. Because the journey is the point, right? Yes, there are times when it would be great to snap your fingers and *be* at the destination, but there are others where you want to enjoy the scenery; play your own little part in the plot unfolding. Good art always affords an opportunity for the latter.

A working title for the track, Kuepper told me, was 'Seventeen Mile Rocks Road Murders', referring to the main road of the suburb just west of Oxley in Brisbane. Seventeen Mile Rocks is such an evocative name for this suburb that, like Oxley, backs on to a bend in the snake-like Brisbane River. Composing this piece brought forth a sense of crime and mystery for Kuepper. Then he had the vision of 'an early Seventies European exploitation film involving this woman Honey Steel ... loosely based on *Honey West*, I suppose, a Sixties spy series ... Having that as an opening theme would be really strong. It wouldn't really matter how good the film was ... '

8   Making *Honey*

I recall seeing Ed Kuepper and Mark Dawson perform as a duo in the mid-1990s at a festival. It was in a vast, tin-roofed building that made every other act sound like various shades of mud. The sense I got of Kuepper and Dawson was of guitars and drums as big as skyscrapers, the songs huge environments with Kuepper's voice as guide. It was a performance that stopped time and from which one emerged feeling changed by an encounter with something that couldn't have previously been imagined. As with much of his recorded work from *Today Wonder* onwards (there are glimpses of this in The Saints' 'Nights in Venice', the Clowns' 'I Don't Know What I Want', and so on), a transformative sense of scale was generated from concentrating on the details of the sound to begin with, then pushing those minimal elements as far as they will go.

There's something slightly intangible about this process, an undefined area between intuition and intent that results in works that continue to intrigue precisely because their effects cannot be defined. Probed about it with respect to *Honey Steel's Gold*, Kuepper circles the idea with statements like:

> I think there is something about the mood of the record that always pulls away a little bit from you. It's hard to explain.

and:

> I wanted it to have this distance, a little bit out of reach, and I suppose that contributes to the fact that you put it on and it doesn't overwhelm you. But it's not an intentional ambient

kind of thing either, it just has a slightly smoky focus, a foggy focus about it.

and more broadly:

> I do strive for something that isn't absolutely straightforward. It doesn't engage me that much if it's really straightforward. It has to be so staggeringly great if it is just a straightforward narrative. Even all the blues music that has a sort of narrative still jumps around. It still has an observation from one perspective, and then it comes in onto something else completely. And I find that that is really evocative. It can be a little confusing, but it's stronger in the long term.

This not-straightforwardness, this smokiness, this mood that pulls away, allows the listener space to live in the music; to roam, to explore, to make their own discoveries. Kuepper spoke to me of seeing b-grade films in the 1970s where the plots often weren't coherent. Sometimes they were exploitation films that had been cut by censors, further eroding whatever sense of narrative may have been present to start with. He received these films, or has long reflected on these experiences, as achieving a space and type of motion beyond literal meaning: 'a pace. It's slightly hallucinogenic … hypnotic, something quite dreamlike about them'.

Honey Steel's Gold, *Black Ticket Day* and *A King in the Kindness Room* particularly present a series of experiments with cinematic framings of songs. In the conversations we've had, Kuepper returns to the moving image as much as recorded sound for reference points, both in the sense of film and TV he consumed when younger, and as someone who probably would have applied his creativity to film-making if he'd been given a chance. One of the reasons that *Honey Steel's Gold* takes us on a series of immersive journeys is that Kuepper often imagined a visual counterpart.

The previous chapter ended with the filmic spectre that hovers around the album's title track. 'Summerfield' also has a celluloid ghost, so to speak.[1] It's worth noting how these tracks, and others from his discography build towards a psychogeography, a personal landscape of the south-western suburbs of Brisbane that continues to haunt Kuepper, or at least figures as a backdrop for many of his imaginings. About the song 'Law of Nature' (from the Laughing Clowns album of the same name), Kuepper writes:

> This kind of refers to Brisbane and in particular, at the time, the semi-rural area where I grew up. Oddly enough even after I'd left there was something in the weather there that continued to exercise a particular potency on me. It had everything you could want – hot sun, broken bottles and people blasting at cats and chickens.[2]

Kuepper imagines a visual counterpart for 'Summerfield' that animates that same landscape, that seems to play upon his imagination as both a composer and a would-be director/cinematographer:

> I had an idea for a film to accompany that, and now that drone technology is fairly cheap, I might even be able to realise it at some stage … It needs the environment in what

---

[1] Or possibly a couple: *Summerfield* is also the name of a 1977 Australian film, a mystery/thriller that concerns a missing teacher and secrets kept by an island community. Thanks to Zoë Carides for pointing this out.

[2] Kuepper, 'Blow by Blow'.

is now Ed Kuepper Park to be right for it, though … Once
you go past the park, you get into this territory where there
are quite a lot of those large power lines. At the right time of
year, you get quite a cracked earth thing happening beneath
them. So I wanted to have something flying over that turf
and around those power lines. I'm not sure if I'll electrocute
myself or bring down the power in Brisbane in the process,
but we'll see …

The park and the powerlines, the hot sun and broken
bottles – it's certainly not a back-to-eden thing Kuepper has
going here. It's a debased, or at least a compromised landscape.
In a sense, the plangent melodies, the transcendence of
Honey Steel's Gold perform a kind of recuperation, not just of a
compromised landscape, but a compromised humanity. At the
risk of getting drippy, Kuepper's art is therapeutic; it provides a
space not where questions are answered but where we might
stop and get a drink; where we might exist for a while in an
environment that provides solace, but not platitudes; where
we can share a wry smile about the downsides of the human
condition rather than attempt the illusion of blocking them
out completely.

Perhaps there's something of this in Judi Dransfield-
Kuepper's understated yet arresting cover image for *Honey
Steel's Gold*. A young woman, or perhaps teenage girl leans
over a small pond, perhaps a shallow depression in the ground
filled by a recent Brisbane downpour. There's no labouring
of the idea of the natural beauty of the landscape; the scene
might be taking place in a paddock by the side of a highway.
If there's a whiff of Narcissus, perhaps equally there's a sense
of critical self-examination, reflection in the cognitive as well
as literal sense, as if the album is a kind of makeshift mirror for
artist and audience alike.

*

While 'Summerfield' is concise, a three-and-a-half minute soundscape, *Honey Steel's Gold* is notable for its epic pieces. 'King of Vice', 'Friday's Blue Cheer/Libertines of Oxley' and the title track account for over twenty-three minutes between them. I asked Kuepper about his predilection for these longer pieces, those that transcend the three-to-four-minute norm that still holds sway in pop and rock. It's something he has been doing since the first Saints album, in the form of 'Messin' with the Kid' and 'Nights in Venice'. Kuepper says:

> There are different types of epic songs. There are ones that have tons of changes – there are a few examples in the Clowns catalogue like 'The Only One That Knows' that goes through a number of different parts. Then there's something like 'Eternally Yours', which is essentially a trance piece. I think 'King of Vice' falls somewhere between the two. It's got an openness about it which means you bring in the verses, the things that hold it together, at your leisure, whenever it feels right.

We get the sense of a confluence of compositional imperatives that help to define Kuepper's work: a tendency towards improvisation as an aspect of structure – indeterminacy baked into sturdy frameworks; a sense of creating moods and environments with an attention to timbral detail rather than straightforward narratives; and a sense of intuition that guides decisions about whether to go for a pop formulation or a more digressive result. Kuepper often tells the story that after the demise of The Yard, someone suggested that he do some solo shows. Thinking this a bit too obvious, he wondered whether playing in a duo with a drummer might provide more sonic scope while allowing for an improvisatory feel. This is why certain blues and folk recordings of the 1940s and 1950s, and certain singer-songwriter recordings of the late 1960s and early 1970s provide something of a blueprint for both *Today Wonder* and *Honey Steel's Gold*. Those documents by the likes of John Lee Hooker, Lightning Hopkins, Fred Neil and Tim Hardin share a *looseness* – a sense of not being locked into strict song-forms, of capturing *performances* that have the freedom to take detours, to stretch and contract, wax and wane. But Kuepper's primal rock influences mean that he brought to this paradigm the orchestral guitar noise of Ron Asheton, of Tony Iommi, of Pete Townshend. Kuepper's albums of the early 1990s represent a remapping, a *distortion* of the singer-songwriter concept.

Pop is far from a dirty word for Kuepper – he talks of thinking in terms of singles for some recordings by The Saints, and his 2021 compilation *Singles '86-'96* demonstrates his mastery of the shorter form. Kuepper acknowledges that *Today Wonder*, *Honey Steel's Gold* and *Black Ticket Day* form something of a trilogy, and to my mind this is because of their delicious sense of looseness and exploration, both in terms of longer pieces (also seen in the contemporaneous Aints albums *Ascension* and *Autocannibalism*) and sonic wonderment. After this the pendulum swung back, and he made two records of more concise song forms, *Serene Machine* (1993) and *Character Assassination* (1994), before getting loose again for *A King in the Kindness Room*. And again, *Honey Steel's Gold* might be seen to effortlessly, unconsciously cover all these bases, with a couple of his lushest epics and a couple of his best-known radio songs finding balance in an eight-track sequence.

*

Kuepper describes the making of *Honey Steel's Gold* as almost an accident.

> EK: What happened with *Honey Steel's Gold* was we were touring in Holland and … I can't remember the name,

just his first name – Paul, who was our record distributor in Holland was really keen on *Today Wonder* and he said: you should record 'Everything I've Got Belongs to You' in a more orchestrated way and we'll put it out as a single here, and it'll be a hit. So we came back to Australia and thinking about that – it was quite different to what I was doing, but I didn't have any issue with doing something that I wasn't doing live. We went in to start recording what was going to be I think a 12" EP, or a 7" single and 12" EP, the way you did things in those days.

And then Paul's record label … somewhere along the line, they stopped being a record label. And suddenly we were like, well what do we do with this stuff? … I mean it's the most unplanned album of my career in a lot of ways. [Hot Records' Martin] Jennings said there's no money in singles, but there is money in albums, so record a few more songs and you've got an LP (laughs). And that's what I did!

JE: It's funny to hear that the genesis of the album is quite ad hoc, because it has the quality of a very well-measured piece of work. Particularly the way it's framed with the extended pieces throughout. Did that have something to do with doing those live shows with Mark Dawson, feeling more freedom?

EK: I think so, we were experimenting with things. A song like 'King of Vice' for instance, that actually goes back to Laughing Clowns days. Originally that little piano intro-duction was played on the saxophone, and I never liked it – I thought it always sounded wrong. There's probably a cassette recording of it around somewhere, and Louise [Elliott] played the introduction. But it didn't feel right. There was something too tense – I could never quite get the band to pull it back in the way it needed to. So with the *Today Wonder* tour, because it was only the two of us playing, it was easy to just throw in songs every now and then and see if they work. So we had 'King of Vice' in that set – on and off, not every night – and started to develop the proper tempo for it. I just used to do the introduction on 12-string guitar, but I didn't like the way that sounded either. Then at some stage it dawned on me that piano had to be the way to go with it – in the same way that the 'Eternally Yours' horn riff was originally written for an organ. Sometimes I think in terms of keys as much as I do in terms of horns.

'The Way I Made You Feel', which is probably the most well-known song on the album, that was played by The Yard … Somebody posted on YouTube a concert The Yard did, I think it's in Switzerland … we play 'The Way I Made You Feel' and probably 'Not Too Soon'. These were songs that were left over that went to make up this album. They'd been sitting around and kind of played in different ways.

And I think *Honey Steel's Gold*, I think you're right, we kind of relaxed our way into it, and I think there's a very cohesive mood on that record … when you say this was never really intended to be an album, that really surprises people. It's got a cohesiveness that comes out of the fact that we had been playing for … I mean the versions of the older songs that had been played by The Yard, they're quite different. It's basically what Mark and I did, and all the other things were put on to complement, to flesh it out a little bit, rather than just have another version of *Today Wonder*, I didn't really want to do that either.

JE: The thing is though, you're talking about it as if it was almost this accidental or unintentional album, but a big part of the artistry is how you put it together once you had the pieces. So regardless of the fact that it started out as a single or an EP and you added more tracks, the conception of the album is having the pieces and going: this is how it fits together …

EK: Oh sure, yeah. I just sort of think it's interesting that in 1990 we went into that first session to make a single for Holland,[3] and we came out with an album that was career-changing in a way (chuckles).

*

A crucial part of the story of *Honey Steel's Gold* is Ed Kuepper finally finding a studio, and engineers, that he could truly collaborate with; that he shared enough common coordinates with that he didn't have to fight to realize his ideas. Adam Chapman first recorded Kuepper for *Today Wonder*, a rebirth warmly received by fans and critics alike. The working relationship would continue for the Aints' *Ascension* and *Autocannibalism*, *Honey Steel's Gold* and the first part of the tracking for *Black Ticket Day*, at which point Chapman decamped for Canberra to begin study that would culminate in a PhD in ethnomusicology. He obviously has a brain for thinking about music in many different aspects, and the four albums he did with Kuepper comprise some of the highlights, he says, of his decade-or-so working as a recording engineer.

Looking back on his discography, Kuepper describes the 1980s as a period where he seldom found that kind of understanding in recording studios. Indeed, among the trials of making *Everybody's Got To*, Kuepper tells me that the engineer

---

3   Almost certainly this would have been mid-1991.

had a habit of replying to any suggestion with the phrase 'cool bananas' – a sackable offence from the perspective of the artist. Proper studio albums (as opposed to compilations) *must* in some way be a product of the time and the circumstances in which they were made. And while we might think of this in terms of the songwriter's emotional state or the dynamics between band members (both relevant of course), those times and circumstances might also amount to a recording engineer's fondness for a certain reverb, or micing techniques, or the (lack of) budget the recording artist has to spend.

For example, Laughing Clowns' debut album *Mr Uddich-Smuddich Goes to Town* contains incendiary performances of fascinating compositions, but sounds at times like it presents the music in quotation marks: there's something of a self-consciousness about, or a lack of awareness of the recording process.[4] *Electrical Storm* has a demo-ish quality about it; both of these records, rather than being compromised, have a certain character that is indelibly mapped on to the material through repeated exposure to the recordings. It is definitely part of their charm – it need not concern us that they don't quite meet the artist's requirements. On the other hand, to my ears the Clowns' *Law of Nature* and the solo album *Rooms of the Magnificent* sound (and I use the term *sound* literally) fully realized, though again each has a specific character. What we might say is that from the time that he started working

---

[4] Writing for the now defunct blog *Life Is Noise* in 2011, Alex Griffin described the album as 'sounding like it was recorded inside Ed's cavernous, musty trachea, the songs are paranoid and shifting, propelled as ever by Jeffrey Wagoner's [*sic*] drumming which sounds like a jittery dinosaur in a Chinese tea room'. Griffin, 'My Top Australian Albums'.

with Chapman, and then Chapman's mentor Phil Punch, the distinct sonic character of each release was something that (i) Kuepper had much more control over and (ii) better, and more consistently reflected Kuepper's personal palette of aesthetics than his recordings of the 1970s and 1980s.

If *Electrical Storm* sounds something like a demo, Kuepper revealed years after the fact that *Today Wonder* was in fact *recorded* as a demo.[5] This reinforced something about his music-making that he had long known, and would repeatedly come back to: an enhanced representation of his live sound at a given point in time would likely result in the sort of artistic statement he was looking for. *Today Wonder* was a studio capture of Kuepper and Dawson's live set at the time. Kuepper is playing twelve-string acoustic guitar through an effects unit, giving it a unique combination of wooden and unearthly timbres, while Dawson had learned to abandon the backbeat and explore the kit – play more orchestrally perhaps – with a cardboard box replacing his bass drum. *Today Wonder* is a documentation of Kuepper rebuilding his house from the ground up. *Honey Steel's Gold* starts from this point and adds judiciously – Chris Abrahams on piano and organ when required, and Chapman and Kuepper working together with the studio as another part of the palette. The album preserves the sense of live-ness and freedom of the duo set-up, but takes a moment to reflect and refine the sonic picture.

In terms of his contribution to the recording, Chapman cites two sources very different from each other. The first is the work of Canadian Daniel Lanois, as both producer and recording artist. Lanois made his name through the 1980s for his work

5   Walker, *Stranded*, 349.

with Brian Eno and U2, but more germane to the kinds of treatments Chapman applied to *Honey Steel's Gold* were Lanois's production of Bob Dylan's *Oh Mercy* and his own debut solo album *Acadie* (both released in 1989). All these works of Lanois evidence an attention to sonic detail, and sonic space; the placing of instruments, particularly guitars and vocals into windows, vistas of reverberation, knitting these individual loci together to compose detailed and immersive soundscapes. Chapman didn't mention it to me, but Lanois's sonic signature also gained great currency through the Neville Brothers' *Yellow Moon* (1989), perhaps the most watery of all these productions. When one critic wrote that *Honey Steel's Gold* sounded like low-budget-Lanois, Chapman was 'quite pleased'.

The other experience Chapman brought to the album was the job that recording dates indicate he probably did directly before *Honey Steel's Gold*: an EP by Sydney band The Moles called *Tendrils and Paracetamol* (1991). There is very little, aside from Chapman's involvement, that the two records have in common. *Tendrils* is free-wheeling, adventurous, somewhat psychedelic, sometimes feral; a compelling record that's a gruesome cousin of the overcast pop associated with the New Zealand label Flying Nun. What the sessions reinforced for Chapman was the creative contribution possible through studio experimentation. As he tells it, The Moles 'weren't a particularly good band musically, in terms of their proficiency, but they were interesting songs. And I went, one of the things to do with this is to try to make it into a soundscape, and to really sculpt the sounds'. It seems *Tendrils* limbered him up to meet the cinematic challenge of *Honey Steel's Gold*.

With Chapman, Punch and Electric Avenue Studios Kuepper found a creative refuge. Aside from a couple of instrumental albums he recorded at home, Kuepper spent a very productive decade – the Nineties – in their company. The strength of the partnership is that, according to Kuepper's artistic vision, it could produce results as varied as the guitar assault of *Ascension*, the quasi-electronic *Frontierland*, the low-key songcraft of *Character Assassination* and the widescreen journey of *Honey Steel's Gold*.

9   The Way I Made You Feel

As Kuepper tells it, 'The Way I Made You Feel' is the hit his record labels couldn't hear. The song had been in the set of The Yard Goes On Forever, and 'it always went over incredibly well live. We were still signed to EMI,[1] and no-one ever came up and said "you've gotta record that, we'll make a hit single out of it."' Even when *Honey Steel's Gold* was released, Hot didn't put their finger on the magic track.

> EK: Y'know, we had the album, we had *Honey Steel's Gold*, and what I think is amusing about it is we had 'The Way I Made You Feel' on it, which was really the song that broke that record. And once again, Hot [Records] didn't put it out as a single. Once again, no-one's actually looking at the song that broke the album. It wasn't until Triple J started playing it, and that was an experience that we hadn't had before, because that coincided with them going national … So it was the first record of mine that actually got heard nationally, and that made a difference. That made the record pick up, sales happening all over the country.

---

[1]   To be exact, Kuepper was signed to True Tone Records for his second and third solo albums (*Rooms of the Magnificent*, 1986 and *Everybody's Got To*, 1988). At the time of *Rooms*, True Tone releases were manufactured and distibuted by Polygram, but by the time of *Everybody's* they had shifted to EMI.

That was great, I remember hearing it walking down the street coming out of people's houses. It happened sometimes, but it wasn't happening much for me in those days. It always struck me as one of those 'oh what's that? That sounds good' before I realised it was me! I know it sounds silly, but it was a kind of disconnect. Once I've done something, I think I kind of move away from it a little bit.

Kuepper doesn't claim to have had the insight himself that 'The Way I Made You Feel' was the one to make an impact … but isn't that what you have record companies for?

'It started when I was cleaning dishes … ' has to be one of the oddest lines with which to start a song. There's the invocation of the domestic – not unknown in pop, but still an unlikely pairing with a slinky, bluesy groove. There's also something of a contribution to the formation of persona here as the protagonist maps on to the recording artist: Ed, the rock star, the guitar-slinger, at the kitchen sink. Perhaps he's wearing an apron. And then there's the wrongness of the description of the action – *cleaning* dishes? Washing dishes, right? There's something unsettling about the whole gambit. I can imagine it falling out of radios around the country, wrong-footing people even as they tap their feet. Yet it's also one of those classic entrees to a story, where the mind is prompted to ask – *what* started when you were cleaning dishes? Of course, we never really find out, beyond the insinuation of 'mass destruction'. And then there's the title, heard repeatedly through the song. It turns these other images on their heads. The protagonist was cleaning dishes – unassuming – and didn't count on mass destruction. This all sounds like a kind of vulnerability: the singer as a passive agent upon whom a calamity is about to fall. But no; it was the way *he* made this other person feel that caused such destruction.

As with 'Everything I've Got Belongs to You' it seems as though our protagonist is a complex of intransigent behaviours. These can be acknowledged as problematic, but are not going to change. There's an inevitability to the damage, the wreckage, if you are to engage. The other line that always stands out to me is: 'There never were good old days as such.' This adds to the image of reluctance to answer the phone due to 'ugly memories of the war'. The protagonist is a realist, and won't tolerate looking at the past through rose-coloured glasses.

So domestic duties give way to some kind of strife. 'The Way I Made You Feel' *feels* so good that you can simply strut around to it, and almost ignore the lyric, until you find yourself singing along to 'I didn't count on mass destruction til I saw you'. It's insidious. The song, the recording does its work on the listener – this seems an inadequate word; the groover? the participant? the co-conspirator? – on a number of levels that are physical, emotional, intellectual, sensual. It gets into you.

'The Way I Made You Feel' is cut from the cloth of the *Honey Steel's Gold* aesthetic in that it unfolds at a stately pace. Kuepper squeezes every drop out of it, with the vocal not appearing until nearly ninety seconds in. The song is built on Kuepper's favourite four-chord trick – I – ♭VII – ♭III – IV for those who read hieroglyphics – and the recording delivers it with an irresistible mid-paced rhythmic glide. It's something like a magnificent old car with big fins doing a slow tour through a neighbourhood, or someone walking at a determined, but unhurried pace toward a rendezvous. The chromatic descent in thirds is the track's indelible hook, memorable and delicious. I think Tarantino missed a trick here.[2]

---

[2]   For what it's worth, Kuepper's nomination for a track of his suited to a Tarantino film is his further extrapolation on the theme of 'Honey Steel's Gold', 'They Call Me Mr. Sexy (Love Theme from "C.C.R. versus the 3rd Reich")'. He also thinks his cover of AC/DC's 'Highway to Hell' would have perfectly suited David Lynch's film *Lost Highway*. Both tracks are found on *A King in the Kindness Room* (1995).

10 *Honey* and 1991, or Ed Kuepper vs. The Biz

1991 was a decisive year in the music industry. After several years in the inner city, Sydney's Ratcat briefly became one of the biggest bands in Australia. Their punk-derived buzzsaw-pop sound had been a major thread of independent music through the late 1980s. Contemporaries The Hummingbirds had paved the way, and the Clouds were poised to make an impact with guitars to the fore but more immersive songwriting and textures. These bands were working (roughly) contemporaneously to Dinosaur Jr in the US and The Darling Buds and The Primitives in the UK, preceded by Hüsker Dü (US) and The Jesus and Mary Chain (UK). Some six months after Ratcat's explosion in Australia, at the end of 1991, Nirvana did the same thing globally, and certain cult sounds forged in underground scenes became the new overground.

Almost overnight, certain barriers between independent scenes and 'the mainstream' were smashed, or so it seemed. In Australia, independent labels got into bed with majors: Red Eye (Clouds, The Cruel Sea), Waterfront (Hard-Ons, former home of Ratcat) and Citadel (Died Pretty, The New Christs) were among those who brokered deals so that artists on their rosters might benefit from new opportunities, and stay with them rather than jump ship. The majors themselves reinvigorated a principle it had long employed: establish an in-house label with zeitgeisty branding and talent scouts close to the ground, or license a label run by industry insiders. This last was the option offered by rooArt. With INXS manager Chris Murphy at the helm, they signed The Hummingbirds, Ratcat, and a bunch of others, and plugged them into the major label machine. A feeding frenzy raged to find the next Ratcat, or Nirvana, or whatever.

1991 was also the year that *Honey Steel's Gold* was released. On the face of things, it would seem perfect timing. Triple J broke 'The Way I Made You Feel' nationally and the album became the highest charting independent release at that time. Kuepper's currency boomed. So, was it just uncanny that this happened when Ratcat were making the jump from cult act on Waterfront to bona fide pop stars on rooArt? Or was there something of a moment when an artist like Ed Kuepper was just a little more likely to find themselves in the charts (albeit the lower reaches)?

Kuepper will have none of it:

EK: What was happening very quickly was once that US discovery of punk, grunge, whatever happened, there were suddenly a lot of boutique labels. So you had this situation where bands would be released on whatever the name of the label was but it was basically a front for EMI or CBS or something. We were actually far more definitely independent, there was no-one else there. The other thing I would say is that I think *Honey Steel's Gold* sticks out like a sore thumb amongst all the grunge. Musically it doesn't overlap with that at all. There was a shift, but a lot of it was actually kind of false, it was the era where everything was being called indie that wasn't Cold Chisel or Midnight Oil.

JE: Or alternative.

EK: Yeah, yeah. I've always hated those names. I don't think any of them apply to me anyway.

As we've noted, Kuepper is the perpetual outsider. While this manifests in various ways, perhaps none is so stark as his relationship to the mainstream record industry. His occasional dances with it have always been kind of awkward. In late 1976, The Saints are signed by EMI in Australia only after their independent single became a sensation in the UK, and EMI UK sent an order to their branch down under. It was a shotgun wedding. The relationship soon soured when Kuepper and co. arrived in London but refused to present themselves as punks – to conform or limit themselves in any way. 'EMI designed their own "Saints suit", a suitably distressed, green garment that understandably was not embraced by the band'.[1] Several years of development in isolation and obscurity, along with the group's determination, meant that The Saints managed to fulfil their three-album quota in eighteen months. If they were underachievers commercially, artistically the legacy is rich. And if EMI lost interest in the group, at least they let The Saints get on with it and achieve their creative goals. The same could be said about the other surprise package they signed – Wire. Both groups presented as something those removed from the scene thought might be punk. Each pursued their own agenda over three albums with EMI that trace an oblivious trajectory of inspiration.

About a decade (and over half a dozen independent Laughing Clowns releases) later, Kuepper signs to True Tone, which releases his second and third solo albums. True Tone was an independent imprint that lasted half a decade and found distribution with a couple of major labels – first Polygram, then EMI. And it was an arm's length association with major capital for all who sailed with them – apart from Kuepper,

---

[1]   Creswell, untitled, 13.

The Go-Betweens, Ups & Downs (Brisbane, Brisbane and Brisbane), The Celibate Rifles, Rockmelons and GANGgajang. As mentioned previously, Kuepper's relationship with True Tone meant that his third solo album *Everybody's Got To* got the benefit of worldwide major label distribution. Kuepper tells this as a comedy of errors, where he and The Yard were always arriving in some town in Europe where the album was yet to be released.

Since then, Kuepper has been in the independent sphere, releasing the great majority of his records through Hot. While he received ARIA awards for Best Independent Release for successive albums *Black Ticket Day* and *Serene Machine* in the mid-1990s (and nominations for a couple more), his next release on a major label was 2015's soundtrack for the film *Last Cab to Darwin*, through Sony.

*

The major label/independent label dichotomy is often taken as a given, but of course, it's more complicated than that. Earlier, I quoted Kuepper's memory of the early 1990s as, rather than independent labels making incursions to the mainstream, of 'boutique labels' that were 'basically a front' for the majors. Looking at the music industry in the UK in the 1990s, David Hesmondhalgh termed these companies 'pseudo-independents'.[2] While he cites the examples of EMI/Virgin offshoot Hut and BMG's Dedicated, this practice goes back decades. Examples include EMI's progressive rock subsidiary Harvest[3] and Phonogram's equivalent Vertigo in the

---

[2]   Hesmondhalgh, 'Indie', 51, 55.

[3]   Curiously, EMI continued the Harvest imprint for its punk/new wave signings in the late 1970s, including Wire and The Saints.

UK in the 1970s. In the mid-1970s following the high sales of jazz fusion artists such as Herbie Hancock and Chick Corea, some US majors briefly set up boutique jazz imprints. A&M had Horizon, Arista had Novus and Freedom.

There weren't actually many (if any) of what Hesmondhalgh would call pseudo-independents operating in Australia around 1990. The distinction may be subtle, but there were two models distinct from pseudo-independents operating in the space between the independent and major label sectors. True Tone is an example of one of these models – where an essentially independent entity hooks up with major label capital and distribution. Through the 1980s, other examples in Australia were Deluxe, which partnered up with RCA, and Regular, who acted on their independence by initially hooking up with Festival, then decamping to WEA for a couple of years before returning to Festival.[4] The towering antecedent for this kind of relationship in the Australian music industry was Mushroom records. Mushroom was independent in its operations but tied to the capital and distribution of the country's only native major label, Festival, from its inception in 1973 until it was swallowed whole by News Corp in 1998.

This indie-major hook-up became a goldrush in the early 1990s, as mentioned earlier with the cases of Red Eye, Waterfront and Citadel, though with its Festival imprint Blue Mosque operating from 1988 to 1991, Citadel were ahead of the game. Red Eye began their arrangement with PolyGram

---

[4] Deluxe released the first two INXS albums, as well as Sydney's Numbers, Perth's Dugites, Dunedin's Toy Love, and Adelaide/Sydney heavy metal band Heaven. Regular had huge mainstream success with Mental As Anything, for whom the label was created, and Flowers/Icehouse. They also signed I'm Talking, the first vehicle for a young Kate Ceberano.

with some autonomy but by the middle of the 1990s it had essentially become a PolyGram imprint – a pseudo-independent.[5]

For the other model, we look to the UK and the US, where larger independents have set up their own distribution networks and retained their independence from the major labels for decades. In fact, their distribution and marketing are so effective that they compete with the majors and break through into the mainstream charts on occasion. These labels, such as Drag City and Matador in the US, and Domino and 4AD in the UK often manage to retain their artists, who seem to have little desire for major capital when the larger indies can both service them with pervasive distribution and guarantee their artistic autonomy.

To some degree, Kuepper found himself in this kind of position with Hot Records around the time of the release of *Honey Steel's Gold*. Although, as Kuepper notes, the album had no connection with prevailing trends, business-wise or musically, it arrived at a confluence of fortuitous industry circumstances. Hot, having just recovered from one of its recurring periods of near-insolvency, secured national distribution with Shock Records in Melbourne. As Mathieson notes, Shock began at the tail end of 1990 distributing three of the bigger Australian indies: Adelaide's Greasy Pop, Melbourne's Au-Go-Go, and Sydney's Waterfront.[6] In 1990, ABC station Triple J, previously broadcast only in Sydney, began its national expansion. So, Kuepper made the record, Hot released it, Triple J began playing it, and Shock were able to capitalize on the groundswell of interest. For once, for Kuepper, everything was

---

5   Mathieson, *The Sell-In*, 146, 206–7.
6   Ibid., 56.

Honey Steel's Gold

in place, and he just happened to make a record that really connected with people. The album made it to number 28 in the national charts during a three-month run. Kuepper asserts that Shock 'credited Nirvana and *Honey Steel's Gold* as being the albums that allowed them to break into a whole lot of new accounts.'[7] Major labels, who needs them?

Kuepper has had his ups and downs with Hot Records over the years; they're no longer associated. What is significant to mention is that Hot got recordings by Kuepper and their other artists (such as The Triffids and Celibate Rifles), released or licensed through the UK and Europe. For a period in the 1990s, they also licensed material to Restless Records, a large independent in the US, including a handful of Kuepper's albums.

As noted, the 1990s was a wildly prolific time for Kuepper, and this manifested itself in a couple of ways. First, there was a succession of albums of new songs: *Today Wonder* (1990), *Honey Steel's Gold* (1991), *Ascension* (1992, by The Aints), *Autocannibalism* (1992, by The Aints), *Black Ticket Day* (1992), *Serene Machine* (1993), *Character Assassination* (1994), *A King in the Kindness Room* (1995) and *Frontierland* (1996). Have you got that? Nine albums of new, song-based material in seven years. It's an incredible run, artistically rewarding and diverse. But from the mid-1990s onwards, things started to get crazy. There

---

[7]   Nirvana's blockbuster album *Nevermind* was released a matter of weeks before *Honey Steel's Gold*. Their debut, *Bleach*, from 1989, was released locally in Australia by Sydney independent Waterfront, and as noted earlier Waterfront was one of the big indies Shock distributed. While *Nevermind* was released in Australia by major label BMG on CD, Shock would most likely have been one of the main importers of the vinyl LP, as there was never an Australian vinyl pressing.

are instrumental albums such as *Starstruck* (1996) and *The Blue House* (1997); there are compilations, both best ofs and b-sides (such as *The Wheelie Bin Affair*, 1997). There are live albums, both solo and with various groups, and an album of covers (*Reflections of Ol' Golden Eye*, 1999). Using *thekuepperfiles.com* as a reference, it seems there were thirteen Kuepper albums released between 1995 and 2000. It was impossible to keep up, and even the most ardent fan must have been asking themselves how many versions of 'La Di Doh' they could possibly need.

While there is something of a pig-in-mud aspect for any artist with the capacity to generate so much material, and a willing pipeline through which to pump it, Kuepper remembers that the reason for such a deluge of material was, in fact, industrial.

> EK: Well, it was chaotic and it was probably because around that time, really, I'd been keeping Hot Records afloat. And even then, that wasn't really enough … I was their biggest seller, pretty much, and they were keen for me to do as much material as possible. Hence the late-Nineties stuff has a slightly eccentric feel to it. It's a box set unto itself, I think.

If the situation with Kuepper's label encouraged him to frame any live recording or set of studio experiments as yet another album, there's nothing to suggest that the artist was following anything but instinct in any of these endeavours.

It would be misguided to think of the music industry as a kind of monolith with intentions or feelings. Or if these exist, it's only in the sense of enthusiasm for things generating hype and money. Otherwise, the default setting of most industry players is, understandably, indifference. If Kuepper has occasionally, briefly, found favour, from a broader perspective the indifference of the industry has served him well. With a tiny infrastructure, he carries on doing what he has done for decades: writing music, making a living through touring, even, increasingly cautiously, releasing new music in physical formats. Perhaps ironically, he has inadvertently cultivated a brand, one that makes up for its lack of ubiquity with a thorny integrity.

11 Not Too Soon/Closer (but Disguised)

'Not Too Soon' is a classic Kuepper pop song in that it pits a disarmingly beautiful melody against a stinging lyric. The first verse finds a character in a sorry state: 'Your unhappiness reached out to me/The acrid smell of sweat gone sour'. In the second, the protagonist's conversation with 'the factory girls' he is liberating – from enslavement or poor working conditions? We're not told – 'was a chore'. In this scattered documentation of unpleasant interactions, there's no narrative; just a dislodging of a couple of burrs that had been stuck in the mind. Somewhat incongruously the music is somewhat heroic, as if negotiating these everyday encounters is much more of a trial than it might at first seem.

Another lyric from the chorus of 'Not Too Soon' sticks in my craw – 'when you talk about destruction'. It's not only a quotation from The Beatles' 'Revolution' (1968), it brings to mind the song we've just heard – 'The Way I Made You Feel' – and its mention of 'mass destruction'. Though Kuepper can be very playful in his songwriting, references to emotional darkness are found throughout his work. If songwriting-as-therapy is a concept a bit too reductive to apply, the working through of life's difficulties is a common process of making any kind of art – just as it is the cornerstone of our dream worlds. To look at something I was saying about fifty pages ago from another perspective, one might say that intuitive creativity comes from the same place as dreams, or somewhere closely related. Each has the potential to uncover new nuances and interpretations through non-linear chains of association (and dissociation); each can enjoy the play of collage, the transference of emotion and insight across realms of meaning and pure sensation.

'Closer (But Disguised)' is the more complex of these apparently lighter pieces. 'Come a little bit closer and forget what you've read', this character asks. Despite (or perhaps because of) 'flames from over the hill', an invitation is extended for reconciliation, to wilfully make two worlds collide (again). Though it would be artificial to try to link all of the songs of *Honey Steel's Gold* into any kind of overarching story – for starters, some are drawn from earlier periods of Kuepper's writing, as I've discussed – we might hear this track as the ornery protagonist of 'Everything I've Got Belongs to You' and 'The Way I Made You Feel' trying to make peace. If there's some unwelcome scuttlebutt doing the rounds, won't you consider that we might transcend that? 'Just assume I understand all that you've said.'

While 'Not Too Soon' is a three-minute pop song, 'Closer' stretches out a bit with a twelve-string acoustic and bass introduction eventually leading into a full band arrangement. There's a simple organ hook playing cat and mouse with the vocals in the chorus and a hammering Abrahams piano solo that sounds like it wants to be a dulcimer. It's a rich mix that has Jon Dale reaching for a comparison with 'the wood-panelled folk of 1970s Witchseason productions.'[1] He may be thinking of Joe Boyd's production of John & Beverley Martin or Richard Thompson, or perhaps Nick Drake's *Bryter Layter*, with its orchestrated folk rock textures.

---

[1]   Dale, 'Ed Kuepper'.

Unlike most of Kuepper's catalogue, 'Not Too Soon' sits in a then-contemporary left-of-centre rock music context, rather than floating adrift in its own alternate universe. That is to say that, to my ears some aspects of this track – chord progressions, certain keyboard sounds – place it in the company of roughly contemporaneous releases by Died Pretty and R.E.M., about which there's more over the page.

For all of its reputation as a layered, atmospheric opus, *Honey Steel's Gold* contains Kuepper's reliable quantum of killer tunes. These two songs arrive towards the end of the album and serve an important structural function. As relatively concise song statements they provide a balance to the longer, more mysterious sonic journeys that have dominated thus far. We're coasting to the closing titles, having a singalong in the back of the car … but periodically aware of the adults having some thinly masked troubles up front.

12 The Wake of *Honey*

One of the things I've tried to do with this book is establish various contexts for *Honey Steel's Gold*. Nowhere is this more difficult than in thinking of what other music was making waves in 1991 and how Kuepper's Klassic might fit. I've mentioned Ratcat and Nirvana and the idea of 1991 as 'the year punk broke' – into the mainstream in Australia and America at least – but I've also agreed with Kuepper that this has nothing at all to do with his work.

I've mentioned Australians Died Pretty and Americans R.E.M. as not a million miles away from a couple of the poppier moments on *Honey Steel's Gold*, and each released a significant album in 1991. For Died Pretty it was *Doughboy Hollow*, considered by many their best. Their post-Velvets/post Patti Smith stormy jangle achieved flights of pure pop and depths of stark melancholy on that record. It's worth noting that *Doughboy Hollow* and *Honey Steel's Gold* were seen as compatible enough that Died Pretty and Ed Kuepper did a tour together in 2008 playing these albums in full. For R.E.M., *Out of Time* completed their transition from college rock cult favourites to one of the biggest rock bands in the world. But listening to these records from start to finish, one has to say that they too bear little resemblance to *Honey Steel's Gold*, which is more elemental, experimental and richly textured than either, while retaining an absolute accessibility. These three albums probably shared a fair cross-section of audience; that's about it.

What else was happening in Australian music in 1991? The biggest selling album of the year in Australia was Daryl

Braithwaite's *Rise*, featuring the deathless hit 'Horses'. Not much overlap with *HSG* there, either. The debut album of the year was Clouds' *Penny Century*, brilliant rock music with teeth, pop hooks for days and a refreshing female perspective. Ditto for lack of overlap. Paul Kelly released *Comedy*, and while he and Kuepper were born in the same year (1955) and at core are Australian singer-songwriters, Kelly has mastered the narrative vignette and the still-life, while the majority of the stuff on *Honey Steel's Gold* is much harder to define. Yes, we can return time and again to *Comedy's* 'Winter Coat' or 'I Can't Believe We Were Married' and read ourselves into those stories laced with simple, emotive melodies. By comparison, we return to *Honey Steel's Gold* as a landscape to be immersed in, to get lost in.

Of Kuepper's direct contemporaries – those Australian figures that emerged in the sonic blizzard of punk to establish significant careers in music, Kim Salmon was in something of a purple patch with his album *Essence* and, released at the end of 1991, The Beasts of Bourbon's *Black Milk*, each in its own way much more bloody-minded and abrasive than *Honey Steel's Gold*. Dave Graney, ex-The Moodists, was on the up. Though mainstream success was still a couple of years away, with drumming and life partner Clare Moore and their group the Coral Snakes he laid the groundwork with *I Was the Hunter … and I Was the Prey* and had already secured a major label deal. His Wild Bill Hickock cabaret schtick was a million miles away from Kuepper. Nick Cave and the Bad Seeds basically took 1991 off as Cave soaked up his new life in Brazil. The Triffids had imploded in 1989 and leader David McComb was struggling to regroup. The Go-Betweens had also hit the fan in 1989, with Grant McLennan and Robert Forster pursuing careers as solo singer-songwriters and Lindy

Morrison and Amanda Brown pursuing a more contemporary pop landscape with Cleopatra Wong.

Perhaps the most significant occurrence in Australian popular music in 1991 was the breakthrough of Indigenous group Yothu Yindi. Their second album *Tribal Voice* and single 'Treaty' would not only put Indigenous music and politics into the upper reaches of the Australian charts, but make an international impact on both festival stages and dance music charts. Through *Tribal Voice*, the holistic, inclusive philosophy of Gumatj leader Mandawuy Yunupingu would influence Australian society and reach out to the world beyond.

I put it to Kuepper that it might be feasible to construct a continuum of Australian independent rock music that has some sense of the elemental. To my ears, Laughing Clowns' *Law of Nature* shimmers with a sense of heat and haze (particularly the title track) that I associate with Australian summers. Perhaps we can hear this in Kuepper's recordings in anything from the heat stroke of 'Messin' with the Kid' to the song-mirages of *Lost Cities*. Ross Gibson – who like Kuepper grew up in Brisbane – heard something like this in 'Electrical Storm'.

> ['Electrical Storm'] encapsulated what goes on in your spirit and in the air when a Queensland storm finally breaks … Here in sonic form is a vivid, distilled world filled with dehumidifiers and massive refrigeration units emitting slow, staticky cycles that help you live with some barely acceptable languor … It was music informed by the environment it came from – the environment *I* had been born and raised in … It was the first time I'd heard my home rendered aesthetically as sound, the first time I'd perceived anything transcendent in the place I'd come from. True, Grant McLennan's marvellous 'Cattle and Cane' had done it already with lyrics, but Kuepper had done it with *sound*. Playing *Electrical Storm* a dozen times, I figured

the transcendence came from the way Kuepper understood
and so vividly communicated the elemental qualities of the
befuddling place that shaped our early years.[1]

Gibson then went back to the first Saints album and realized
he had missed a similar resonance from 'Messin' with the Kid':

Yep – there it was, way back then, the subtropical rock
aesthetics … less perfectly wrought than in *Electrical Storm*
but sly and brilliant all the same: the revelation of a torrid
but torpid teen-angst, *localised*, exhausted, uninterested in
looking up and focusing on productivity or big-city energy:
the sonic rendition of a habitat and of a people who are
never going to be at the centre of attention …[2]

Though not specifically subtropical, I have these kinds
of experiences with The Triffids' *Born Sandy Devotional* and
certain records of the 1990s by The Cruel Sea and The Dirty
Three. Each of these artists is distinct from the other, but to my
ears they share that sense of elemental shimmer that I imagine
to be quintessentially Australian. There's a sense of drone in
The Triffids' songs such as 'Wide Open Road', 'Lonely Stretch'
and 'Field of Glass' that have you suspended in a luminous,
somewhat hostile landscape. Anwen Crawford writes that
'Wide Open Road' is

a song that shimmers with summer light even as it traces out
a winter of the heart, a song vast enough to fill the horizon
yet intimate enough to feel as if it were being played right
beside you. I would wager that there are few pop songs so
beautiful as 'Wide Open Road', though perhaps its magic is

---

[1]   Gibson, 'Subtropical Rock', 122–3, italics in original.

[2]   Ibid., 123–4.

only wholly palpable to a listener who holds within them a sense of what this country feels like: its heat, its distances, its fraught and haunted spirit.[3]

The sure-footed grooves and rippling guitars of The Cruel Sea are not unrelated to this sense of sun. The harmonic simplicity and sense of improvisation at the heart of The Dirty Three, equal parts plaintive and explosive, might also be heard as having a precedent in *Honey Steel's Gold*. After checking that *Law of Nature* was released before *Born Sandy Devotional*, Kuepper cautiously allowed that this continuum might, indeed, be a thing.[4]

*

There isn't room here to cover the thirty-plus years of Kuepper's career post-*Honey Steel's Gold* in detail, though I have mentioned many of his recordings of this period along the way. As I've noted, his recording output slowed to a trickle

---

[3] Crawford, 'One of the Great Australian Albums'. I acknowledge that this perspective on an Australian elementalism is a broad brush, and in distinction to Gibson's Brisbane-specific musings.

[4] To be fair, being from Perth and crossing the Nullarbor repeatedly for sorties into the Eastern states, The Triffids have their own brand of Australian elementalism. Although I've indicated examples where they create soundscapes to evoke this sense, it also appeared literally, in the lyrics of early tunes such as 'Place in the Sun' (1981) and 'Spanish Blue' (1982). Jon Stratton has written on the particularity of The Triffids'/David McComb's songwriting in the sense of it articulating a suburban moral code. This itself is particular to the group's origins in Perth, a city both wedged between the forbidding environments of sea and desert, and devoid of a true inner-city that might spawn expressions less in thrall to a moral conservatism. See Stratton, 'Suburban Stories', and *Australian Rock*, 173–98.

in the new century. After *Smile … Pacific* (2000), there was a long break from the release of new material. Three CD sets were released, summing up major spans of Kuepper's output: *All Times through Paradise* (2004), four discs that assemble the complete Kuepper-era recordings of The Saints 1976–8; *Cruel But Fair: The Complete Clowns Recordings* (2005), everything Laughing Clowns released, spanning 1980–5 on three CDs; and *This Is the Magic Mile* (2005), Kuepper's three-disc selection of his recordings of the 1990s.[5] With a seven-year gap between albums of new material, the focus of the 2000s seemed to be the past.

When *Jean Lee & the Yellow Dog* did finally arrive in 2007, it seemed something of an explosion of pent-up creative energy. It canvasses a number of styles, instrumental combinations, and even production gambits. It was a welcome challenge for his fans, and with its loose concept relating to the last woman hanged in Australia, intersected with the country's history in a way that created further intrigue. It's the only time (since the days of The Saints) that Kuepper has co-written an entire album with another person; in this case his wife Judi Dransfield-Kuepper, who contributed the bulk of the lyrics.

---

[5] Caveats: (1) In the works is a box set based on The Saints' *(I'm) Stranded*, which promises previously unreleased mixes and live material; (2) Laughing Clowns' first film-clip is for the song 'Just Because I Like'. Although the song was re-recorded at the sessions for *Ghosts of an Ideal Wife* (appearing not on the album but a contemporaneous single), the original 1979 recording of the song used for the film-clip has not been otherwise issued. (3) Conspicuous in its absence from these box sets is Kuepper's output from 1985 to 1989: the first three solo albums and various singles and EPs. In a 2004 interview, Kuepper told me that the period was already adequately represented in compilations. Though he did not specify this, it would seem he was referring at least in part to *The Butterfly Net* (1993).

Recent years have seen a recovery of mojo, or perhaps more of a willingness to engage with the machinery of releasing records. Three releases show the continued breadth and cohesiveness of Kuepper's music-making. 2015's *Lost Cities* is a solo record of new songs, the atmospheric approach of which will be familiar to those who have seen his solo (and duo) shows since the late 1990s. The guitar is discernible, if shrouded in a sonic fog, the music gentle but foreboding. 2018 saw the release of *The Church of Simultaneous Existence* under the name of The Aints! This project ran for a few years as a live entity and involved reconfiguring material written for The Saints. The album was largely of songs that had not previously been recorded, making for a canny intersection of past and present, with a sound extending from The Saints' *Prehistoric Sounds* with its mix of garage rock, soul and even jazz.

Jazz keyboardist and composer Alister Spence had occasionally guested with Kuepper for many years before being part of The Aints! In 2019, Kuepper performed with the Alister Spence Trio. The music was completely improvised, and a recording session resulted in an extraordinary double CD of work by the quartet, *Asteroid Ekosystem* (2020). As we've seen, Kuepper has always been interested in improvisation: we can hear this everywhere from the Stooges-ey blowouts on the first Saints album, through to the looseness of the soundscapes on *Today Wonder*, *Honey Steel's Gold* and *Black Ticket Day* and the Aints' early 1990s albums. *Asteroid Ekosystem*, it would seem edited from longer jams in the fashion Spence sometimes employs with his trio, charts its own course through ambience, jazz, noise, rock and minimalism, not as a menu of styles so much as a seamless new genre that may touch on any of these and more. Lloyd Swanton on double bass, Toby Hall on drums and glockenspiel, Spence on keyboards and at times electronics, and Kuepper on his expanded guitar rig blur the boundaries of their respective instruments. At times the sound seems electronic, at others it is highly percussive. Again, the spacious terrain of *Honey Steel's Gold* might function as a reference point for, if nothing else, Kuepper's contribution to the musical atmospheres.

Disrupted by Covid-19 cancellations, Kuepper's 2021 tour as a duo with drummer Jim White extended well into 2022. White is perhaps best known as part of The Dirty Three but is a collaborator *par excellence* across a myriad of contexts. As he seems to in all his twenty-first-century projects, Kuepper effortlessly fused multiple phases of his career in these shows. The guitar-and-drums duo brings to mind the pairing with Mark Dawson on *Today Wonder*, but White's free and at times flamboyant relationship to the kit is closer to Clowns drummer Jeffrey Wegener than Dawson. Kuepper includes several Laughing Clowns tunes in the duo sets with White, transforming them into shapes both atmospheric and improvisatory, in some senses bringing together elements that made *Honey Steel's Gold* so evocative. The classic Clowns' composition 'Collapse Board' was a hair-raising, spine-tingling centrepiece of both shows I saw in 2022. Kuepper's guitar sound has that processed element – the timbres can be expansive and somewhat orchestral, or distorted and somewhat remote. It's as if a variety of distorting funhouse mirrors are applied to the guitar and Kuepper is going to take you on a magic carpet ride regardless of whether you would like to hear something that actually sounds like a guitar. But this means the music also connects to his late 1990s experiments with guitar timbre, as well as the explorations with Asteroid Ekosystem.

If you immerse yourself in what the artist himself sometimes refers to as The Exploding Universe of Ed Kuepper, there's an elastic web of Kuepper-plasma, a cosmic signature. The connections to various parts of Kuepper's career I've found in the Kuepper-White duo shows are a feature of every release of his. Each speaks to various strands of his musical investigation. Each supplies a piece of the grand Kuepper tapestry. Each creates a concise experience that works within its own parameters. And it's no coincidence that *Honey Steel's Gold* is among his most successful and most-loved albums, because it's one that reconciles so many of these threads. To paraphrase Neil Young, all of his changes are there.

13 Summerfield

it tumbles it's music that revolves electric and electronic and imbued with an Ed-ly essence a hurdy-gurdy and a horse and cart a wooden box with strings something flying overhead and bumping over rocks and hillocks at once a sacred vessel a humble transport a court musician playing a simple air for your pleasure a bagpiper turning over and over in a tumble-drier the radiation from the overhead wires melting the frost drying the dew from your toes your life coming to a peaceful conclusion guitars spinning gold gossamer the clowns faces turning side to side forever laughing with you not at you a feeling of all-encompassing warmth as the sun does its work without being asked bright yellow red and blue flowers sucking in the summer you can feel them reaching ever higher the bees humming the tune over and over making honey and are those flutes maybe recorders how are they made of steel and wood at once steel and wood at once (there are no flutes there are no recorders certainly no hurdy gurdy) wire and hair and grass and broken bottles the rays bouncing off them and resonating across the expanse perhaps it's last drinks as the sun sets and we are at the end of the day's labour these machines are capable of much but we use them for peace they watch over us with loving grace they generate gentle chimes that spin round and round forever we know they keep going even when we can no longer hear them and the shadows begin to stretch they get tall and we taller with them and the yard does indeed go on forever except it is not quite a yard there are no fences no sense of land claimed or contained what it is is a field a field in summer a summerfield

References

Bongiorno, F. (2015, 2017). *The Eighties: The Decade That Transformed Australia*. Carlton, VIC: Black Inc.

Brooker, W. (2019). *Why Bowie Matters*. London: William Collins.

Crawford, A. (2016). 'One of the Great Australian Albums: The Triffids' *Born Sandy Devotional* 30 Years On'. *The Monthly*, https://www.themonthly.com.au/issue/2016/february/1454245200/anwen-crawford/one-great-australian-albums, accessed 27 August 2022.

Creswell, T. (2004). Untitled liner note to The Saints box set *All Times through Paradise*. EMI Australia.

Dale, J. (undated). 'Ed Kuepper'. *Shfl*, https://theshfl.com/guide/ed-kuepper, accessed 11 July 2022.

Encarnação, J. (2008). 'Bastard Country, Bastard Music: The Legacy of Australian Punk'. *Sounds of Then, Sounds of Now: Popular Music in Australia*, edited by Shane Homan and Tony Mitchell. Hobart: ACYS (Australian Clearinghouse for Youth Studies, University of Tasmania), 199–214.

Gibson, R. (2006). 'Subtropical Rock'. *Meanjin* 65 (3), 119–24.

Griffin, A. (2011). 'My Top Australian Albums', https://web.archive.org/web/20141017175602/http://lifeisnoise.com/2011/06/28/my-top-australian-albums/, accessed 3 August 2022.

Hesmondhalgh, D. (1999). 'Indie: The Institutional Politics and Aesthetics of a Popular Music Genre'. *Cultural Studies* 13 (1), 34–61.

Ingham, J. (1976). 'Singles'. *Sounds*, 16 October, 37.

Kendall, A. (2021). 'Meet: We Chat with the Legendary Ed Kuepper (The Saints, Laughing Clowns, The Aints) about His Long and Distinguished Career, Setting Parameters as an Artist and Continually Learning'. *Backseat Mafia*, 26 April, https://www.backseatmafia.com/meet-we-chat-with-the-legendary-ed-kuepper-the-saints-laughing-clowns-the-aints-about-his-long-and-distinguished-career-setting-parameters-as-an-artist-and-continually-learning/, accessed 18 July 2022.

Kuepper, E. (2004). 'Blow-by-Blow Reflections on Each Track by Ed Kuepper'. Liner notes to *Cruel but Fair*. Sussex and Annandale: Hot Records.

MacFarlane, I. (2020). 'Ed Kuepper | Long Play Series'. *Australian Music Vault*, https://www.youtube.com/watch?v=9We_NGcTeB0, accessed 28 July 2022.

Marcus, G., ed. (1979, 2006). *Stranded: Rock and Roll for a Desert Island*. 2nd edition. New York: Da Capo Press.

Mathieson, C. (2000). *The Sell-In: How the Music Business Seduced Alternative Rock*. St Leonards, NSW: Allen & Unwin.

Nichols, D. (2016). *Dig: Australian Rock and Pop Music 1960–85*. Portland: Verse Chorus Press.

Pottinger, P. (2004). Untitled liner note *to Cruel but Fair*. Sussex and Annandale: Hot Records.

Reynolds, S. (2005). *Rip It Up and Start Again: Postpunk 1978–1984*. London: Faber and Faber.

Stafford, A. (2004). *Pig City: From the Saints to Savage Garden*. St. Lucia, QLD: University of Queensland Press.

Storey, J. (1993). 'Ed Kuepper: From Saint to Aint'. *Bucketfull* [sic] *of Brains* 42, 11–15.

Stratton, J. (2007). *Australian Rock: Essays on Popular Music*. Perth: Network Books.

Stratton, J. (2009). 'Suburban Stories: Dave McComb and the Perth Experience'. *Vagabond Holes: David McComb and the Triffids*. Fremantle: Fremantle Press, 35–43.

Street, A. P. (2017). *The Long and Winding Way to the Top: Fifty (or so) Songs That Made Australia*. Sydney, Melbourne, Auckland and London: Allen & Unwin.

Thompson, S. (2007). '1975 Ed Kuepper's Valeno Guitar', https://www.migrationheritage.nsw.gov.au/exhibition/objectsthroughtime/edkuepperguitar/index.html, accessed 28 July 2022.

Walker, C. (1996, 2021). *Stranded: The Secret History of Australian Independent Music, 1977–1991*. Revised and expanded edition. No place of publication given: The Visible Spectrum.

Wilsteed, J. (2016). 'John Wilsteed Chats with Ed Kuepper', https://www.youtube.com/watch?v=lNZ_Be_iM_g, accessed 8 July 2022.

Index